A WAKE-UP CALL FOR MAINSTREAM AMERICA

SARAH PALIN'S
PIECE OF THE AMERICAN
PIE

ROSEMARY E. BACHELOR

PENTREF PRESS 2010

This book is lovingly dedicated to

Catherine Amanda Moore (Foust) Merrow

Who believes in looking for the wizard behind the curtain

and to

William Henry Merrow

Who turned over his birthday toys and demanded,

"Mom, why is everything made in China?"

CONTENTS

PREFACE

Alaska! Two of my great-uncles, Frank and Lou Carpenter, were Klondike gold miners at Wiseman, Alaska, where their sister, Clara, later joined them to teach a largely Eskimo student population. My parents took to the AlCan Highway in a retro-fitted VW wagon in the late 1950s but had to charter a plane to visit Wiseman. This outpost above the Arctic Circle was not accessible by road until the 1990s. In 2000, its population was twenty-one. The census area for this community covers seventy-eight and one-tenth square miles!

I picked up Sarah Palin's book, *Going Rogue*, read one chapter and wondered why this all sounded like the 1950s, when I was a teenager. When I realized why, I was troubled by the questions it raised. These questions were uncannily related to concerns I have had for the past two decades. They touch on such serious subjects as patriotism, war, feminism, a forgotten piece of advice from President Eisenhower, preserving our planet, vagaries of the American economy, the faith of every American, keeping the church out of my bedroom, and what today's religious leaders think about Eve and the apple.

I, too, have a religious background. I love my warm, supportive faith community, which worships at the oldest Anglican cathedral outside the British Isles. I am also an ordained deacon in the Old Roman Catholic Church, an offshoot of the Roman Catholic Church that ordains women to the priesthood and permits clergy to marry. I believe in God, in separation of church and state, don't think the government should tell me what to do with my body and/or my sexuality, and have a different definition of patriotism than Ms. Palin.

I find it unsettling that our nation's leaders are talking trash about each other. What many feared was happening is now confirmed. Our representatives in Washington are so busy jockeying for power that solutions to urgent problems facing America are no longer a priority.

Yet, these serious problems need the undivided attention of all of our elected officials. Their constituents deserve nothing less.

Answers to some of my questions have an ominous undercurrent that threatens the underpinnings of the American Constitution, suggest that Sarah Palin is either a clever chameleon or a victim, and call into question whether or not a majority of American voters could likewise be victimized. There is a lot of finger-pointing going on, but are any of the fingers pointing in the right direction?

There is one major question that remains unanswered. It is about the authenticity of the now notorious, celebrity-style Sarah Palin. It either has a very simple one sentence answer or an extremely complex one. It needs to be answered for the American electorate before the next presidential election. America's future could be at stake.

Rosemary E. Bachelor
West Melbourne, Florida

http://www.sarahpalinanalysis.com

ACKNOWLEDGEMENTS

My gratitude to Joanna Woodson Foust, a loving companion who continuously supports me in meaningful ways and who gave proof-reading help and editorial guidance for this project.

My heartfelt thanks to members of the Anglican Parish of Quebec, who worship at the Cathedral of the Holy Trinity. They are a powerful support network for each other and offer prayerful concern when things go awry. For me, they are like an extended family.

CHAPTER ONE

SARAH PALIN: AN APPLE PIE LIFESTYLE

"If you want to make an apple pie from scratch, you must first create the universe." ~ *Dr. Carl Sagan*

In grandmother's day a patriotic, religious wife and mother was described as Bible bred, corn fed, and as good as apple pie. There was more. It all fits Sarah Palin to a tee.

That was then. This is now. Sarah Palin operates in the now and that old fashioned description doesn't work anymore. Or does it?

The 1950s were the postwar decade when America underwent huge changes. Men had left the farms of rural America during World War II knowing little about the rest of the world, both at home and abroad. After the war and having seen so much more of the world, many never went back to the farm.

It was an era of prosperity. Good jobs were available in the more populated areas. This was the impetus that gave rise to the great American migration to the suburbs. This was not, however, the case in Alaska.

In the 1950s, most Americans had a fairly common idea of what Bible bred meant. Religious? You either went to church or you didn't. You read the Bible or you didn't. You turned up in church on Sundays or played golf, went on a picnic, or drove to the grandparents for the every Sunday family dinner instead.

Corn fed? That's long been associated with being wholesome. The image is of an outdoors person who is healthy and strong. It has been associated with ruddy cheeks or a tan. It originally pertained to children who grew up on farms in the Midwest Bible belt and left the rural scene to work in town. They were called corn fed by city dwellers. The term fell out of use after hundreds of thousands left the farms and suburbia came of age.

After patriot Samuel Adams went on a picnic in 1697, he entered his startling menu in his diary: "Had first Butter, Honey, Curds and cream. For Dinner, very good Rost Lamb, Turkey, Fowls, Applepy."[1] That's one of the earliest American references to apple pie.

The "as American as apple pie" metaphor, however, had its birth in the nineteenth century and meant "typically American." More recently the Apple Marketing Board of New York used "As American as apple pie" as a slogan. When journalists asked World War II American soldiers why they were fighting, they often replied "for mom and apple pie."[2]

Sarah Palin, in many ways, is like a throwback to the 1950s. She seems much more familiar to today's grandmothers than their own grandchildren or great-grandchildren. She talks the way folks did in the 1950s. Describing women who staffed the Right to Life booth at the 2008 Alaska State Fair, she calls them gracious *ladies*. Ladies?[3] That's a word that grates on many feminists' ears. Ladies! It is often a patronizing term used by men. There is nothing wrong with this word choice. It probably seems natural in Alaska. In most of North America, however, the word has become outdated. Females are called women.

Alaska has remained so undeveloped that when Sarah Palin won the Wasilla mayoralty, the town had dirt streets and was known for its Iditarod mushers. It was the home of duct tape renegades. What are those? Do-it-your-selfers who use duct tape to patch their boots and numerous other things. When Wal-Mart finally got to the Wasilla that mushroomed during Palin's leadership, the Wasilla store broke the record for duct tape sales. Wasilla was named honorary world duct tape capital.[4]

This is Sarah Palin's milieu, and her comfort zone. In fact, she doesn't fit well outside it. The rest of the country is more like a foreign country to her.

ALASKA'S '50S LIFESTYLE

The events and values of 1950s America helped shape that era's lifestyle. More than traces of that lifestyle remain in Alaska. It's like a time warp. Palin will tell you that many families stock their freezers with meat from animals they have hunted and killed.

The behind-the-times progressive socialization of Alaskans, much of it a causal factor in Palin's political philosophy and executive decision making, does not offer much experience in dealing with issues in what Alaskans call "the lower forty-eight," although there are some ironic parallels.

Palin wouldn't push a salary hike for the previous Wasilla mayor she served under as a council member, noting that until there were funds for upgrading roads, the mayor's salary didn't need an upgrade. That's when Wasilla still had dirt roads.

At the same time, all across America, deteriorating bridges and highways from long ago decades were overdue for redoing. As Alaska pays for its newly needed infrastructure, most other states are trying to figure out how to pay for infrastructure updates or replacements.

THE GLORIOUS 1950S

What were the 1950s like in the rest of the United States? Here are some glimpses. The economy was at a healthy growth rate and new housing proliferated in suburbs that were popping up on the outskirts of nearly every major city.

The Korean War ended, Fidel Castro created the first communist government in the western hemisphere, and the Cold War between the United States and Russia gathered momentum. Sputnik 1, the world's first satellite, was launched by the Soviets in 1957. It was also a decade of decolonization. The Belgian Congo and other African nations gained their independence from Belgium, France, and the United Kingdom. Cambodia and Laos gained independence. Formation of North Vietnam and South Vietnam, however, would lead to a long war that began as the decade ended. Shortly after its formation, the People's Republic of China invaded Tibet and intervened in the Korean War. Germany was divided and Soviet bloc nations were effectively cut off from the West by what Winston Churchill termed an "iron curtain"; the Soviet Union dominated eastern Europe.[5]

The U.S. presidents of this era were Harry Truman (1945–1953) and Dwight D. Eisenhower (1953–1961). A burgeoning rise of materialism became a driving force in the lives of ordinary Americans. Two-car families emerged. Children's allowances more than tripled.[6]

THE ROLE OF WOMEN

This was the age of the happy homemaker. Most wives were stay-at-home moms. Domesticity was idealized in the media. Marriage and children were part of the national agenda, much as they are in Palin's. Between 1940 and 1960, the number of families with three children doubled and the number having a fourth child quadrupled.

Many young wives, however, weren't content to face three decades of childbearing and did something Sarah Palin would consider a no-no . They started taking the pill.

The media pictured Soviet women in drab clothes working in even more drab factories, their children packed off to cold Communist day care centers. In contrast, American women were pictured with feminine hairdos and delicate dresses, as they tended the home fires and enjoyed the fruits of capitalism, democracy, and freedom.

The U.S. marriage rate was at an all-time high, and women who went to college went for what many of their fathers considered an M.R.S. (pronounced Mrs.) degree, i.e., a husband with earning power. In *Going Rogue*, Sarah reports that as a high school senior, she prayed that God didn't have a local boy in store for her because they all seemed like brothers to her.[7] Indeed, she recounts that she had about given up hope that she would ever meet a boy she would like as more than just a buddy. Then Todd Palin moved to Wasilla because it had a good basketball team and he was too good for the team at the school he attended in the town where he grew up.

In the 1950s, girls who weren't married by twenty-five were considered to be in danger of becoming old maids. Being single and pregnant was considered totally unacceptable. Unwed mothers were shunned.

Although young women were expected to remain virgins, many didn't, and the demand for easy, safe, and reliable contraceptives grew but not yet as fast as in following decades. It is interesting to note that objections to contraceptives during the 1950s, when several states had laws prohibiting or restricting their sale or advertisement, were not the same as now. Instead of this being a right-to-life issue, the long entrenched view was that using contraceptives was lewd and immoral, and promoted promiscuity.

MEDIA AND THE ARTS

Most American families began the 1950s without owning a television set and ended the decade with at least one set. Television would revolutionize news dissemination, the world of entertainment, and how Americans used their leisure time. Some of these changes even made their way to Alaska but primarily in the culture of its largest cities. With a big push from TV exposure, Elvis became the teen idol of the 50s, thanks to hip-grinding, pelvis-gyrating, and guitar-swaying TV performances that some parents thought were too sensual. *Howdy Doody Time*, *I Love Lucy*, and *Dragnet* were hits. Rock 'n roll resounded at high school sock hops across the nation. Rhythm and blues and country music gained in popularity. Perry Como crooned, Judy Garland captured hearts, and Ella Fitzgerald added a new range to soul music.[8]

Lego toys were born just as the decade began, Silly Putty eggs sold by the millions, matchbox cars were invented in 1954, and Barbie hit the shelves in 1959. Peanuts was born in 1950, and the first issue of *Playboy* hit the stands in 1953. We laughed at Bob Hope and Groucho Marx and cried to "Cold, Cold Heart" and "The Tennessee Waltz." It was the decade of *The Asphalt Jungle*, *High Noon*, *My Fair Lady*, *West Side Story*, and *The Sound of Music*.[9]

Although the 50s were primarily a decade of normalcy and conformity, artists and poets broke the mold. Abstract expressionism was a new art genre. Beat Generation poets strayed into open verse forms and political issues.

Cars traveled faster on new highways, and soon billboards replaced the seven thousand Burma-Shave signs that dotted the American landscape.[10]

At a 2008 Anchorage women-against-Palin rally, R.D. Levno, a retired school principal, flew in from Fairbanks. "She's a child—inexperienced and simplistic," she said of Sarah. "It's taking us back to junior high school. She's one of the popular girls, but one of the mean girls. She is seductive, but she is invented." Do you know the type? [11]

PROFILING ALASKA

Approximately half of Alaska's 698,473 residents live within the Anchorage metropolitan area. As of 2009, Alaska remains the most sparsely populated state in the United States.[12]

Alaska has been identified, along with Pacific Northwest states Washington and Oregon, as being the least religious in the nation. According to statistics collected by the Association of Religion Data Archives, about 39 percent of Alaska residents were members of religious congregations. Evangelical Protestants had 78,070 members, Roman Catholics had 54,359, and mainline Protestants had 37,156. After Catholics and Eastern Orthodox, the largest single denominations are the Church of Jesus Christ of Latter Day Saints (Mormons/LDS) with 29,460, Southern Baptists with 22,959, and Orthodox with 20,000. The large Eastern Orthodox population (with 49 parishes and up to 50,000 followers is a result of early Russian colonization and missionary work among Alaska natives.[13]

Economically, Alaska is unique. It imposes practically no taxes on its citizens, but levies the oil industry to boost the state's financial coffers. This is such a successful money stream that Alaska has a huge surplus in reserve that allows it to distribute rebates to its citizens.

Ah, the glorious 1950s! They ended just before the turbulent 1960s and 1970s, decades of inner strife—the civil rights movement—and, the far away and the widely protested Vietnam War that couldn't be brought to an end.

Sarah Palin was born soon after the 1950s ended but grew up in an isolated Alaska landscape only partially permeated by what made news in "the lower forty-eight,"

AMERICA'S GROWING PAINS[14]

Something was going on in the rest of the United States that had little impact on Alaska. It was the civil rights movement.

Many who were then young adults look back on the civil rights movement of the 1960s and1970s as a time of painful reckoning. White Americans, most with European ancestry, were increasingly confronted with the specter of a subclass of black Americans beginning to protest the poverty to which they had been relegated and the lack of education, skills, and equal rights that made them unable to compete in the American work arena.

Black Americans, too, had left the rural South during World War II. Many were in the American military, where some earned the respect of fellow white soldiers for their bravery and heroism. Many blacks in the military were also taught new skills. When the war ended, there was no future to be had in going back to the rural South to live as a poor sharecropper or house servant.

There was another group of blacks that left the rural South during the war. Many of them were women and middle-aged men. They found jobs up north or in California, often as salaried factory workers. Almost every large American city had an influx of blacks during and after the war. Before long, there were black ghettos in places like Detroit, Chicago, Philadelphia, Newark, and New York. African Americans also moved to small industrial towns like Benton Harbor, Michigan, home of Bendix and other manufacturers, and Plainfield, New Jersey, a town from which many executives commuted to New York, as well as a community that employed many blacks in menial jobs serving wealthy families.

By the 1960s, there were more educated blacks, some of them thanks to the G.I. Bill. Their incomes enabled them to have purchasing power, and they began to move into middle class neighborhoods where they often were not welcome.

THE CIVIL RIGHTS MOVEMENT

During the 1960s, nonviolent protest actions, primarily characterized by civil disobedience, led to confrontation between activists and government authorities. Federal, state, and local governments, as well as businesses and communities, faced crisis situations that emphasized inequities faced by African Americans. Forms of protest and/or civil disobedience included sit-ins, boycotts, and marches.

Although leaders, inspired by Martin Luther King, insisted on the type of nonviolent protest used by Gandhi in India, the opposition was under no such constraint, and violence erupted during the 1965 Selma to Montgomery marches. One black and two whites were killed. Television watchers across the nation saw police and state troopers brutally beat bloodied marchers.

President Lyndon Johnson was among the TV viewers. He reacted immediately by personally submitting to a joint session of Congress what became the Voting Rights Bill. He said:

> What happened in Selma is part of a far larger movement which reaches into every section and state of America. It is the effort of American Negroes to secure for themselves the full blessings of American life. Their cause must be our cause, too, because it is not just Negroes but really it is all of us who must overcome the crippling legacy of bigotry and injustice. [15]

The struggle continued. There were more casualties. Martin Luther King was assassinated three years later and immediately race riots broke out in more than 100 U.S. cities. Race riots continued and the black power movement gained momentum. It enlarged the aims of the civil rights movement to include racial dignity, economic and political self-sufficiency, and freedom from oppression by white Americans.

The day before King's funeral, his widow and three sons, and approximately 20,000 people marched through the streets of Nashville. Many carried signs that read Honor King: End Racism. National Guardsmen lined the streets, some manning M-48 tanks. The next day 150,000 joined the King funeral procession in Atlanta.

It took years of affirmative action programs and other causal factors before African Americans had a role in government, gradually holding elective offices in their own communities, as well as in county, state, and national governmental positions. They also attained management level positions in the state and federal bureaucracy, as well as prominence in all professions.

In retrospect, it was the right to vote that brought African Americans into the mainstream, particularly in the South, where they were a majority in many counties. The 1965 act suspended poll taxes and literacy tests. It allowed federal examiners to replace local registrars where voting discrimination persisted.

Within months of the act's passage more than 250,000 new black voters had been registered, one third of them by federal examiners. Within four years, voter registration in the South had more than doubled. Blacks regaining the power to vote changed the political landscape of the South.

When Congress passed the Voting Rights Act, only about 100 African Americans held elective office, all in northern states. By 1989, there were more than 7,200 African Americans in office, including more than 4,800 in the South. Counties of majority black population saw white sheriffs who had abused blacks replaced by black sheriffs. Before long, there were black mayors in Jackson, Mississippi, in Atlanta, and in New Orleans. Now blacks serve in the U.S. Congress and on the Supreme Court. Colin Powell was an army general and the U.S. Secretary of State.

TODAY'S PERSPECTIVE

We now have two-plus generations of Americans that didn't experience the civil rights era of the 1960s and affirmative action measures of the 1970s that guaranteed African Americans seats in college classrooms and the upward mobility that eventually placed black people in the highest jobs and offices in the nation.

It is probably difficult to envision blacks having to sit at the back of the bus or not being allowed to use the same drinking fountains and lunch counters as white citizens. At the time of the first Selma-Montgomery freedom march the population of Lowndes County, Alabama, was 81 percent black and 19 percent white, but not a single black was registered to vote. At that time there were 2,240 whites registered to vote in the county, a figure that represented 118 percent of the adult white population. How so? The names of white voters were retained on the rolls after they died or moved away. That was but one of many illegal practices in an era when Ku Klux Klan members took the law into their own hands and not only brutally beat up blacks, but destroyed their homes and hanged them for minor offenses.[16,17]

"I have a dream," Martin Luther King said. Part of his dream is now sitting in the White House. When Barack Obama was elected president, many felt that the United States had finally come of age, had reached maturity. It only took a few weeks to see that this was not so. Untrue rumors swept the online community like a raging fire. People posted slanderous, libelous, and hateful comments about their president. Civil rights legislation may have brought bigoted racists under the thumb of the law, but it didn't remove the hatred from white supremacists and other unhappy factions. That hatred is once again near the boiling point. Membership in hate groups has risen dramatically since Obama went to work in the Oval Office. People who profess to be born-again Christians have ignored Christ's plea for inclusiveness in the New Testament and the Old Testament admonition to love our neighbors.

Sarah Palin grew up thousands of miles from race riots, civil rights marches, and legislators formulating laws that guaranteed equal rights to all Americans, regardless of race, color, or creed. Probably Sarah, her parents, and her siblings did not have to determine how they would deal with African Americans at work, at school, or as neighbors. They were not challenged, as white Americans, to decide whether or not, in their dealings with black people, they would follow the Biblical admonitions or be hypocrites—whether they would eagerly uphold the civil rights laws or silently rebel.

When Sarah Palin was mayor of Wasilla, Alaska (1996–2002) the town's racial makeup was 85.5 percent White, 5.2 percent Native American and 0.59 percent Black/African American, with a small number of Asian residents and a few of mixed Caucasian and native American background. There were 5,469 residents.[18]

Although she grew up in an area removed from racial tensions and race riots, as Wasilla mayor, Sarah Palin had an African American constituent who knew all about the civil rights era. Mahala Ashley Dickerson (1912–2007) of Montgomery, Alabama, was a lifelong friend of Rosa Parks, a heroine of the civil rights movement. Dickerson became Alabama's first black female attorney. Later, the divorced

Mahala homesteaded in Alaska with her triplet sons, became Alaska's first black attorney, spent her later years in Wasilla, and was still practicing law in her early 90s.

"All men are created equal." "Government by consent of the governed." "Give me liberty or give me death." And those are not just clever words, and those are not just empty theories. In their name Americans have fought and died for two centuries and tonight around the world they stand there as guardians of our liberty risking their lives. Those words are promised to every citizen that he shall share in the dignity of man. This dignity cannot be found in a man's possessions. It cannot be found in his power or in his position. It really rests on his right to be treated as a man equal in opportunity to all others. It says that he shall share in freedom. He shall choose his leaders, educate his children, provide for his family according to his ability and his merits as a human being.

Rarely in any time does an issue lay bare the secret heart of America itself. Rarely are we met with a challenge, not to our growth or abundance, or our welfare or our security, but rather to the values and the purposes and the meaning of our beloved nation. The issue of equal rights for American Negroes is such an issue. And should we defeat every enemy, and should we double our wealth and conquer the stars, and still be unequal to this issue, then we will have failed as a people and as a nation. For, with a country as with a person, "what is a man profited if he shall gain the whole world, and lose his own soul?"[19]

~ Lyndon B. Johnson, March 15, 1965

CHAPTER TWO

SARAH PALIN'S RELIGION:BAKED IN WHICH OVEN?

"I like your Christ, I do not like your Christians. Your Christians are so un-like your Christ." ~Mahatma Gandhi

Sarah Palin's mother, the former Sally Ann Sheeran, was born into a large, educated Catholic family who lived in Utah, where her father, Clem (short for Clement), was a General Electric mediator. When Sarah was an infant, her mother was active in the Catholic Church in Skagway, Alaska, where they lived until Sarah was five.

THE DIVERGING FAITHS

Chuck Heath, Sarah's father, had little interest in organized religion, but he and his wife agreed that the children should attend Sunday school. During the family's early years in Wasilla, Alaska, Sarah's mother attended the Catholic Church but also was a weekend volunteer Presbyterian secretary who became involved in mission work with northern Eskimo villages. Sally (Sheeran) Heath then reached beyond the liturgy, theology, and Roman Catholic Church itself, accepting a friend's invitation to try an Anchorage evangelical church.

Sarah and her siblings were attending the local Assembly of God Sunday school, which Sarah described as the most "alive" one in Wasilla. It often is the case in small towns that there is one Sunday school that is more popular than the others and friends of its Sunday school students gravitate there even though their parents may attend other churches. These are often the Sunday school programs that have special activities in addition to the Sunday meeting or that sponsor summer Bible camps and other wholesome activities for children and initiate programs geared for teens.[1]

It was at a summer Bible camp at Alaska's Big Lake that Sarah made a meaningful personal connection between Alaska's awe-inspiring beauty and the Creator into whose hands she would put herself, relying on trust and faith to lead her onward. She and her siblings were baptized in Big Lake's chilling waters, and a young Sarah began reading her Bible the first thing every morning and the last thing each night.[2]

TOGETHER: FAITH AND FREEDOM?

Sarah's entire family was deeply involved in various sports. Even her mother became a marathon runner. Just as she had tied nature and the creator God together, Sarah forged spiritual links between sports and her practice of religion. Some of this imprinting came from the local Fellowship of Christian Athletes, which she and the high school wrestling coach led. Some sixty or so members conducted Bible school in public school classrooms and had motivational discussions that inspired them to work harder and to focus on goals.[3]

Sarah makes an interesting remark about this in *Going Rogue*. She says this was before American Civil Liberties Union (ACLU) "activists" told young people to "feel offended" when other people exercised freedom of religion.[4]

The ACLU position, however, would most likely be that the real subject in the context of any such ACLU message would be separation of church and state, meaning that the issue was not over the free exercise of religion but religious activities included in a taxpayer-supported public institution.

As a teen testing ideas and trying to form a *persona* leading to a mature adulthood, Sarah was surrounded by a secure world in which patriotism and freedom were taken for granted. The heights of experiential patriotism and freedom were Memorial Day weekend and the Fourth of July weekend. Flags and bunting draped homes, main street shops, and public buildings in much of small town America. Most places had parades, with floats, marching veterans, and high school bands. Faith and freedom went together and for Sarah may have been connected to the extent that she saw freedom as a gift from God. For her, that could be a natural, logical conclusion.

What Sarah was not exposed to during her Alaska upbringing was a shadow across much of America, where millions of people, both black and white, did not feel fully free. Blacks were still victims of racism, particularly in the rural South and in northern ghettos. Poor white people living in places like Appalachia were victims of grinding poverty that made them feel servile and worthless. Many did not have the education or training to enter occupations that afforded them a chance to own their own homes and adequately provide for their families. For them, freedom meant a chance to live a more privileged and productive life.

For those who grew up under these shadows, both as victims and witnesses, freedom did not appear to be a gift from God, given to everyone at birth. For the disadvantaged who believed in God, their God was a God of hope and mercy. There was a deep chasm between faith and freedom.

APART: CHURCH AND STATE

There are some who believe what is most wrong with the religious right is its attempt to unite church and state. If you put this in the patriotic context of the foresight of the founding fathers, right-wingers will still insist that you are wrong, and they are right.

Sarah's colonial ancestors came from families who left England to settle in America because a religious mix ceased to exist in the British Empire. These people were victimized if they did not adhere to the government-imposed faith. Yes, *the* faith—one faith in the form of one government-determined church structure. Some of Sarah Palin's ancestors were among the *Mayflower* pilgrims who came to America, so they could worship as they pleased. In Virginia, where most of the original colonists were merchant-adventurers, the situation was different. These colonists brought their Anglican religion with them to the New World; it was the forerunner of the American Episcopal Church.

Freedom of religion is a very important constitutional issue that deserves to have constant attention from generation to generation. It requires discussion, elucidation, careful consideration, and an involved electorate that tries to understand what led the founding fathers to insist upon separation of church and state.

Do we have politicians who are looking to the Bible to justify their actions in secular matters that affect a citizenry of many religions, including some whose central core is not based on the Bible? Shouldn't politicians charged with governmental responsibilities instead be looking to the Constitution for guidance?

The Rev. Barry Lynn, a United Church of Christ minister and a constitutional attorney, is among clergy who insist the United States must continue to separate church and state. He became executive director of Americans United for Separation of Church and State in 1992. His nationally syndicated radio show *Culture Shocks with Barry Lynn* can be heard at www.cultureshocks.com.

Rev. Lynn builds a cogent case around the thesis that religion, when united with the power centered in government, gives birth to tyranny. He goes two steps further:

1. The separation of church and state is really an important and effective ally to religion. When government doesn't mess with religion—and only then—religions have prosperous growth.
2. Religion doesn't need government's assistance, and it is inappropriate to teach it in government-financed schools.

This leads to an observation. One of Sarah Palin's heroes is Ronald Regan, whom she often quotes. One of those quotes is: "America is still the abiding alternative to tyranny. That is our purpose in the world—nothing more and nothing less."[5]

Rev. Lynn concludes that when radicals from the religious right attack separation of church and state, they are really attacking the freedom of religion mandated by the Constitution's First Amendment. How so? Because they ultimately wish to impose their faith on all of us. Rev. Lynn has been crusading against the religious right for a long time. In his book *Piety & Politics*, Rev. Lynn lays out in great detail how the religious right could undo freedom of religion for Americans.[6]

Notable Americans have praised both Rev. Lynn's book and his crusade against what he believes is an effort by religious right radicals to destroy separation of church and state because, quite simply, they don't believe in it.

Phil Donahue: "*Piety and Politics* summons the silent among us to rise up and, with a firm voice, support the constitutional separation of church and state. Barry Lynn reminds us that our own one-of-a-kind founding document is a powerful stiff arm against the tyranny of the righteous, the 'called,' who insist on writing your child's biology text-books, public funding of private schools, placing Jesus on the wall of public buildings, condemning homosexuals, disallowing a choice in family planning, and working every day to reestablish America as a nation of one faith, *theirs*."[7]

Nadine Strossen (president, ACLU): "Relying on common sense, as well as his expertise, Barry Lynn convincingly makes the essential point that mixing religion and government does not benefit religion."[8]

SARAH PALIN'S TAKE ON RELIGIOUS FREEDOM

The crucial question about Sarah Palin's take on religious freedom is whether it is the radical version or instead one that incorporates the basic precepts of the founding fathers. Put another way: Is Sarah com-promised by right-wing radicals who claim they can get her elected to national office or is her view more tempered and perhaps more simplistic?

Here is an important question: Does Palin believe this because it was told to her or because she is familiar with constitutional history, has thought this all through, and has then arrived at her own conclu-sion in a justifiable way?

There is also middle ground here. Palin says that everything she ever needed to know she learned on the basketball court. Basketball and other sports do teach some of life's lessons, especially that of building and leading a successful goal-oriented team.

Sports, however, do not teach constitutional history nor give one an opportunity to carefully examine it. It is then possible that Sarah Palin has not had enough exposure to the complexities of the American Constitution and can easily be forgiven for not knowing what led the founding fathers to be so definite about separation of church and state.

DOES GOD BELONG IN THE OVAL OFFICE?

The United States has had numerous presidents who were devout Christians. Some have had leadership roles in their denominations. Yet, they didn't visibly mix politics and religion beyond the point of showing by their actions and deeds that their faith had made them moral, upright, and honest individuals who treated other people with compassion, had a sense of honor, and believed in fair play and other virtuous acts of dealing with the welfare of the American people.

It was not until the presidency of George W. Bush that people started to question a president's brand of Christianity.

It was on the night of that terrible Sept. 11, 2001 that many Christians began to wonder about God's role in the life of President Bush. It was because of the context in which the president placed both of them.

Quoting Psalm 23, Bush declared that the day's horrendous events were for Americans but the first phase of a new act in the cosmic struggle of good versus evil. When queried about this response from the man who Americans regarded as a president, not a prophet, government officials, and Bush supporters said this was nothing new. Many presidents, they said, had mixed politics and religion.

Because Palin, too, mixes religion and politics, this is an issue to examine. First, what makes both of them different from former presidents is not their belief in God or how many times they refer to God in their public communications. Roosevelt, Reagan, Carter, and Clinton, as well as many other presidents, all referred to God in their inaugural addresses and other public speeches.

What makes Bush and Palin different is what they say when they do talk about God. It's that prophetic overtone. It is the stance that they are interpreting God for Americans or passing along the creator's advice.

Presidents have commonly spoken of God in an intercessory way, asking for God's blessing on the American people and their country or requesting the deity's guidance for themselves because of the great responsibilities they carry. Often, it is an expression of humility.

Bush veered from the path when some of his pronouncements were presented as echoing God's wishes or even as warnings for not only our nation but for the whole world. Historically, there have been countries in the world that have leaders who do audaciously act as God's messengers, but these are not typically nations who practice a democratic form of government and treasure liberty and freedom. Ironically, the best example of a contemporary country run by the pronouncements of a religious leader who acts as a voice of God is Iran, which both Bush and Palin have been quick to criticize. In the case of Iran, the people knowingly handed power over to a religious leader.

Bush wasn't—and Palin isn't—a recognized religious leader. No part of the presidential job description lists ability to interpret God's wishes as a qualification.

Early on in the "War against Terrorism," Bush embarrassed us globally with a line he drew in the sand: "Either you are with us, or you are with the terrorists." This is the type of either black or white thinking typical of many political and religious fundamentalists. It is so characteristic that they become defensive when their "logic" is questioned. This simplistic approach is also a root cause of their other war: the war on intellectuals that Sarah Palin vigorously champions to the point that she doesn't even try to hide it.

Whether or not they regard themselves as intellectual or highly educated, most Americans see how easy it is to go from the with-us-or-against-us terrorism pronouncement to "either you are with us or you are against God."

This latter rationale is not acceptable to millions of American Christians and members of other religions who are not fundamentalists. It is offensive to people who are not churchgoing Christians, but do believe in God or another supreme power. America has always guaranteed freedom of religion. That is one of the cornerstones America was founded upon. Another of those cornerstones is separation of church and state.

There is another reason to go beyond this black and white method of reasoning. The rest of the world is watching and many of these onlookers have posed a serious question. How does one distinguish between the position that either you are with us or you are against God and the nearly identical message of the terrorists we are fighting? Listen to Osama bin Laden speak, it's apparent he believes he and fundamentalist Muslim followers are engaged in a holy war and that they are carrying out God's wishes to punish the United States for its materialism and other perceived sins. What message is our nation communicating? Is it one most Americans are willing to support? Here is something to contemplate:

"Clearly, flying airplanes into buildings in order to kill innocent people is an indefensible immoral activity. So, too, is an unprovoked pre-emptive invasion of another nation," say David Domke and Kevin Coe, who have written about President George W. Bush's "Brand of Christianity."[9]

Domke and Coe point also point out the cost in casualties for Iraqi civilians and military, as well as those of U.S. soldiers sent to fight because of incorrect intelligence, concluding "That isn't freedom and liberty, no matter how many times you use the word or link it to God."

SARAH PALIN AND DOMINIONISM[10]

Sarah Palin and *dominionism* have been appearing in the same sentence with increased frequency. This is one of those times when uneducated people with lazy minds are using *dominionist, dominionism*, and related terms any way they want to, without understanding the difference between what the words imply and what they really mean. The following insight is given by Chip Berlet, a senior analyst with Political Research Associates and an author who covers civil rights and civil liberties. When it comes to dominionism, he is an expert. Berlet, along with Sara Diamond and Fred Clarkson, helped popularize the term *dominionism*. He says: "I feel an obligation to clear up this confusion, which stems from some very sloppy research posted on a number of Web sites where the terms 'Dominionism,' 'Dominion Theology' and 'Christian Reconstructionism' are used improperly and interchangeably." For starters, according to Berlet, "Sarah Palin is a 'Dominionist' with an apocalyptic End Times theological viewpoint that sees the war in Iraq as part of God's plan." Neither Sarah nor the Assemblies of God church she attends, should, says Berlet, be characterized as practicing a form of "Dominion Theology" or "Christian Reconstructionism. That would, he insists, be wrong. Much fairer would be suggesting that Sarah "displays the tendency called 'Dominionism' in some of her public statements."

Are we going around in circles here? Not necessarily. The starting point is a 1994 speech Rev. D. James Kennedy gave at the 1994 Christian Coalition national convention. Kennedy described "true Christian citizenship" as a societal commitment to "take dominion over all things as vice-regents of God." In reporting on this speech and, later, in discussing a growing political tendency in the Christian right, sociologist and journalist Sara Diamond popularized the term *dominionism*. Diamond carefully discussed how the small Christian Reconstructionist theological movement had helped introduce 'dominionism" as a concept into the larger and more diverse panorama called the Christian Right. "Dominionism is therefore a tendency among Protestant Christian evangelicals and fundamentals that encourages them to not only be active political participants in civic society but also to seek to dominate the political process as part of a mandate from God," Berlet writes.

The supporting Biblical text is Genesis 1:26 in which God discusses man as created in his image to have dominion over all living things on earth. Most Christians read this and think God appointed them stewards of earth. It is something they can do with humility as part of their faith. However, some Christians read this scripture and believe that Christians alone are mandated to occupy all secular institutions until Christ returns. This latter approach is the idea of dominionism.

The Christian right is the general category into which all these separate groups belong, the reconstructionists being the most radical. Diamond believes reconstructionism is intellectually grounded. Only the more intellectual leaders get involved in the theology and, no matter how much Sarah Palin pooh-poohs intellectuals, they are components of the Christian right movements. Berlet calls Christian reconstructionism a form of theocratic dominion theology. Its leaders, he says, are challenging evangelicals across a wide spectrum of theological beliefs to get more muscular about political involvement.

It would be helpful to know how much distance there is between the reconstructionists and the increasing number of boots-on-the-ground people being inspired by Palin to "take back America," whatever that means. So far, little of Palin's hype has characterized where she stands on reconstructionist theology. The public doesn't even know if she understands the differentiations made by Diamond and Berlet.

It seems almost certain that people supporting Palin in a "take back America movement" can't be focused solely on wresting secular leadership positions away from their present occupants so they can move into them. That's not what some segments of the Christian right are envisioning. Those who want to build a theocracy would make second or third class citizens of people who don't share—and prac-tice—their religious beliefs. So, if Joe six-pack doesn't go to prayer meeting and doesn't know the Bible better than any other book he's read, he'll get left behind. Many of the leaders in this movement don't tolerate alcoholism, filthy language, or feminists. They also believe in punishing people for their sins. The goal is to impose a biblically grounded morality on everyone on earth, no matter what his or her belief.

TWO DEFINITIONS: SOFT DOMINIONISTS AND HARD DOMINIONISTS[11]

"Soft Dominionists are Christian nationalists," according to Berlet. "They believe that biblically defined immorality and sin breed chaos and anarchy. They fear that America's greatness as God's chosen land has been undermined by liberals, secular humanists, feminists, and homosexuals …Their vision has elements of theocracy, but they stop short of calling for supplanting the Constitution and Bill of Rights."

"Hard Dominionists believe all of this, but they want the United States to be a Christian theocracy," Berlet explains. "For them the Constitution and Bill of Rights are merely addendums to Old Testament Biblical Law. They claim that Christian men with specific theological beliefs are ordained by God to take over society."

Where does Sarah Palin register on this vast scale of difference among members of the Christian right? If it is the extreme recon-structionist theology, then the United States government could be reshaped as a religious society. It would be headed by religious lead-ers, much as Iran is today. In Iran, thousands of people have recently publicly defied Iran's religious regime. Why? Because it has taken away their rights and severely curtailed their freedom.

There are millions of devout Christians in the world who are not fundamentalists or members of the Christian right. Instead of advocating the world be run by the punitive Old Testament moral codes of a vengeful God, they base their lives on the more humanistic precepts of the New Testament and the compassionate ways of a loving God. Many of them do not think religion and government should be blended together to govern a nation. They do not see how this is possible without sacrificing democracy.

Sarah would tell you she has been born again—saved. Yet one wonders what is the centerpiece agenda for her religious faith. We live in an era in which some religious Christians point at other religious Christians and attack them in very base, gut-level ways. One hopes that if Sarah Palin does have aspirations for nationwide leadership that she will not rally her supporters around pronouncements that President Obama is a Nazi and other sensational stories denigrating the first African American president of the United States.

There are many pronounced conflicts in Sarah Palin's account of her religious motivation. As we follow step by biographical step in *Going Rogue*, we encounter some minor inconsistencies about Sarah Palin's religious fervor. For example, she thanked God when Todd Palin arrived in her life, but she was not married in a church. There was a considered decision to elope, with neither family nor friends present when she and Todd tied the knot.

THE MARRIAGE OF RELIGION AND POLITICS

Some onlookers, many of them in Canada and the European nations, sense in the United States an unstable marriage of politics and religion that projects a very fundamentalist worldview. Its wedding cake is decorated with incendiary ideas for domination of the Mideast, ideas that intrigue Jews and terrify Muslims.

Many sideline observers of Sarah's upward and onward trajectory express concern about all the things she doesn't know. It may, however, be time to be disturbed about what Sarah appears to believe. Here is a look at those things that can be classified as part of her faith and her religious or spiritual life.

Palin attended the Wasilla Assembly of God Church from age ten until about six years ago. The Assemblies of God is the world's largest Pentecostal denomination, with more than sixty million members worldwide. Its four cornerstone beliefs are:

- Salvation through Jesus Christ
- Baptism in the Holy Spirit
- Divine Healing
- The second coming of Christ

What started as a pacifist denomination has become one of the major militaristic pockets of Protestantism. Here are some of Sarah Palin's involvements.[12]

- Evangelist Bill Gothard envisions a "First-Century Kingdom of God" with conversion taking place one city, one state, one school board, one police force, and one mind at a time. The movement hosts conferences designed for city officials to enter its one-city-at-a-time program. As Wasilla mayor, Sarah attended at least two of those conferences. This movement is a reconstructionist view of Christianity that believes separation of church and state are the cause of social ills.
- Many Pentecostals advocate dominionism and think Christians must take control of the world's governments and resources to prepare for Jesus to return and reign over earth. Palin's pastor asked believers to pray that Alaska be a home to Christians during the end times. Speaking at her church, Palin said: "I believe Alaska's one of the refuge states…in the last days. And hundreds and thousands are gonna come to the state to seek refuge."
- The end times: Many evangelical Christians are waiting for the return of Jesus or for a fiery apocalypse in which only faithful Christians are saved. The Assemblies of God believe the end times are happening in the current generation. (They have believed that for more than 100 years.) Palin has participated in end times discussions and a longtime

associate allegedly told *Salon* that Palin told her "I think I will see Jesus come back to earth in my lifetime."

- Palin sometimes attends Wasilla's Church on the Rock, which recently sent its youth group to training for Joel's Army, a movement that uses militaristic rhetoric to inspire young people to convert people in anticipation of the return of Jesus. Palin tried to obtain Alaska state grants for a Juneau youth center that uses some of the same language as this end-time youth army, which is looking for "revolutionary believers."

- While governor, Palin spoke at the Master's Commission graduation ceremony at Wasilla Assembly of God. This was the speech in which she discussed God's plan for Iraq. The Master's Commission program is a replacement for college studies. Its young Christian adults focus on prophetic gifts, prayer, evangelism, and scripture reading. The Master's Commission discipleship training program is often run by pastors prominent in the Joel's Army movement.

- Three churches attended by Palin are involved with the "Third Wave of the Holy Spirit," a large and growing militant evangelical movement. Third Wave "apostles" think they hear directly from God and have a divine mandate to form a worldwide church for the end times. The Wasilla Assembly of God, Palin's church for more than twenty-five years, has a strong connection to this movement and the head of "Jews for Jesus" has spoken there. (Some Third Wave adherents believe Jews must be converted to Christianity to realize God's plan.)

THE SUMMING UP

Many people fear the handing over of any federal government leadership role to Sarah because she often talks about what God says about our nation (it is going to have to pay for its sins) and because they think that if she had a momentous decision to make, it would be a simplistic one attributed to God, the ultimate decision maker, and would ignore the advice of knowledgeable advisers.

Our summing up here is from two sources: 1) Rev. Dr. Welton Gaddy, leader of the nonpartisan grassroots interfaith alliance and pastor at Northminster (Baptist) Church in Monroe, Louisiana, and 2) Sarah Palin herself.

"Enter Sarah Palin, the driver at the wheel of a political vehicle that has catapulted out of control. Obviously Sarah Palin does not know enough about the road of democracy or the rules for driving it." ~ *Rev. Dr. Welton Gaddy*

Frightened, anxious people are being hurt by Sarah Palin's distorted version of American history and perverted view of the future, according to Rev. Dr. Welton Gaddy.[13] He is executive director of the Interfaith Alliance, a faith-based organization of over fifty different religious traditions, with over 100,000 members who are committed to promoting the positive and healing role of religion in our society. It actively opposes the manipulation of religion for political goals.

Rev. Gaddy was astounded when Palin, in response to a federal court ruling, told a Louisville, Kentucky crowd that a judge had ruled that a government-celebrated National Day of Prayer was unconstitutional and, said Palin, "America needs to get back to its Christian roots." Sarah Palin, he said, "cannot distinguish between fanciful images of revisionist historians and actual facts documentable in the chronicles of the nation's archives."[14]

Sarah has said that George Washington is her favorite founding father. However, she apparently has not read much about him. *"The government of the United States is not in any sense founded on the Christian religion."* That's George Washington speaking, Rev. Gaddy points out, noting that Washington's successor, John Adams, after signing a treaty with a mostly Muslim nation, repeated Washington's comment nearly verbatim.

Palin, who is on record as an ardent supporter of the First Amendment, in throwing her hissy fit about a federal judge's decision that the National Day of Prayer is unconstitutional, just doesn't get it. She seems oblivious to the fact that the judge's decision was based on that First Amendment to the Constitution! By contrast, many theologians, divinity school professors, and pastors nationwide were happy to have a judge who understood the First Amendment's religion clauses.

It's what Rev. Gaddy called that rush to the microphones by "bandwagon religionists" to declare "the further moral ruination of the nation" that is disturbing. Palin found the ruling "mind-boggling," and Gaddy found Sarah's alarmist rhetoric equally mind-boggling.[15]

Palin was right in pointing out that the founding fathers were believers, Gaddy said, but he doubts their religious identity in any way resembles that of Palin's Pentecostal evangelical tradition. Rev. Gaddy makes this point about the founding fathers: "The larger truth is that these were people, regardless of their religious identity, who had witnessed the abuse and violence that emerge when institutions of religion and government became entangled."[16] Palin and her ilk, Gaddy says, "represent danger to religion and government because "they understand neither the freedom for everybody at the heart of real religion nor the religious freedom assured by the Constitution."[17]

Americans do not need their president to tell them when to pray or what to pray for, Gaddy says, explaining that prayer is often private and voluntary. "But neither do the American people need Sarah Palin stirring a revolt to get rid of the very principles that have assured efforts to guarantee civil rights to everybody and made our nation great," Rev. Gaddy warns.[18] His conclusion? "It is, indeed, like watching a car wreck that has just happened or is about to happen. It is time for more of us to scream, 'Watch out!'"[19]

Sarah Palin has many times spoken of her religion—her practice of it, and what it means to her. Her religion is such a big part of her life that she has difficulty disassociating herself from it. There are references to it in nearly everything she writes and in most of her speeches. Following are some of her expressions of her thoughts about the role of God in her life and in the world. They are direct quotations, each followed by abbreviated source citations.

- Pray for our military men and women who are striving to do what is right. Also for this country, that our leaders, our national leaders, are sending them out on a task that is from God. That's what we have to make sure that we're praying for, that there is a plan and that that plan is God's plan. (Sarah Palin's June 8, 2008 address to the graduating class of commission ministry students at Wasilla Assembly of God, Palin's former church in Wasilla, Alaska. It is in the context of her son Track, 19, being deployed to Iraq.)

- I can do my part in doing things like working really, really hard to get a natural gas pipeline, about a $30 billion project that's going to create a lot of jobs for Alaskans, and we'll have a lot of energy flowing through here. And pray about that also. I think God's will has to be done in unifying people and companies to get that gas line built, so pray for that. (Same June 8 address)
- I think we should keep this clean, keep it simple, [and] go back to what our founders and our founding documents meant. They're quite clear that we would create law based on the God of the Bible and the Ten Commandments. It's pretty simple. (Appearance on the TV program *The O'Reilly Factor*, May 6, 2010)
- That will be the position I will be in as long as I'm on earth— that is, seeking the right path that God would have laid out for me. (Q&A with *Time* magazine's Jay Newton Small, Aug. 14, 2008)

Sarah Palin again mistakenly implied that our nation's Founding Fathers, including George Washington, were against separation of church and state in an April 16, 2010 address to the Women of Joy conference in Kentucky. Here's what she told those evangelical Christian women:

I beg you, Women of Joy, to bring light and be involved, loving America and praying for her. Really, it is our solemn duty. Praying for true spiritual awakening to overcome deterioration. That is where God wants us to be. Lest anyone try to convince you that God should be separated from the state, our Founding Fathers, they were believers. And George Washington, he saw faith in God as basic to life.

She's right. They believed in God and were devout Christians. They did, however, strongly believe in separation of church and state.

CHAPTER THREE

AT ISSUE: THE INGREDIENTS

"God always has another custard pie up his sleeve" ~ *Actress Lynn Redgrave*

"America is ready for another revolution!" Sarah Palin told the crowd. That was the first of several standing ovations she received from Tea Partiers at their Nashville convention in February of 2010.[1]

You didn't have to be there to know what other issues brought the crowd to its feet. Most of America knows the Palin litany: people are to have guns but not have abortions. We should ramp up the war in the Mideast, extending it into Iran, but we should trim the budget deficit that helps pay for it.

Let's look at many of the issues Americans are concerned about and see where Sarah fits in.

SARAH'S "FOREIGN POLICY DEBUT"

Sarah Palin is on an International Speaker's Bureau list and one of her initial high-paying speaking engagements was in Hong Kong in September 2009. The press, which was not invited to the closed-door event, dubbed it her first speech overseas and saw it as an avenue to counteract her perceived lack in foreign policy experience. It was perhaps a start at obtaining foreign policy credentials even though the subject was the global financial picture. That being the case, you can bet she didn't prepare her own speech.

Her audience was described as Asian bankers, investors, and fund managers. The word *Asian* was meant to refer to the location not the persons attending. Many represented financial groups from the United States, Canada, and numerous other places outside Asia. Persons attending the speech declared Palin to be well prepared and articulate. She spoke about ninety minutes from prepared notes, but the understanding was that she would not accept questions afterward. Her speech was described as balanced and wide ranging.[2] Although not critical of President Obama, whom she described as "*our* president," Palin did express concern about large federal bailouts in the banking and automotive sectors and the large federal government deficit. There was a reference to rebuilding the Republican Party from the grassroots, but persons interviewed after the speech did not feel she was speaking as a far right, ultra-conservative Republican. Palin also spoke of Tibet, Burma, and North Korea as places where China should be more sensitive about human rights issues. Randy Scheunemann, former foreign policy adviser to presidential candidate John McCain,[3] accompanied her.

Palin did not represent the American government, so it is difficult to assess how significant her content was for investors interested in an advance peek at where the American economy is headed, or how important the Chinese government rated her remarks about Tibet, etc. Despite the facts that the book contract that made her a millionaire overnight and that she has for several years lived lakeside with an airplane parked in the driveway were in the news, she described herself as "someone from Main Street U.S.A."

Some Palin watchers have observed that Palin may be at her best when talking about money matters. That is the area in which she claimed success as mayor of Wasilla and governor of Alaska and she is known as a fiscal conservative.

The Hong Kong event was sponsored by CLSA Asia-Pacific Markets, Asia's leading independent brokerage and investment group. In December of 2009, CLSA Books published Richard Duncan's second book, *The Corruption of Capitalism: A Strategy to Rebalance the Global Economy and Restore Sustainable Growth*. Duncan also addressed the conference. His book gives a comprehensive explanation of the causes of the economic calamity that began in 2008 during the Bush Administration. It has three parts: Part I describes the present state of the global economy and the government life support keeping it afloat. Part II details the long series of U.S. policy mistakes responsible for this disaster. Part III outlines what it will take to restructure the U.S. economy and restore global economic growth.

Duncan, who predicted the financial collapse in a 2003 book[4], has worked for brokerage houses, the World Bank, and the International Monetary Fund. He claims the current multitrillion dollar government intervention is all that is preventing a worldwide breakdown on the scale of the Great Depression and the economic crisis in the United States means Asia's era of export-led growth is over. "In terms of the direction of asset prices in Asia, and around the world, they will be determined by the size and timing of successive rounds of government stimulus packages in the United States and within Asia. The global economy will remain on government life support for years to come," Duncan said.[5] He, too, addressed a session of the Hong Kong gathering. Indeed, the 2009 CLSA conference in Hong Kong sounds more like a place Sarah Palin could gain valuable insight than a place where she could contribute any of her own expertise.

WHY KID GLOVES FOR ISRAEL?

American religious fundamentalists have often gone on record as supporting Israel. This is in line with their Bible-based view of the world in which Israel continues to be treated as "the promised land." Without knowing much about Israeli politics and both the root and continuing causes of the Israeli-Palestinian conflict, many Christians feel a brotherly kinship with their Israeli counterparts.

These fundamentalists indeed appear to have more affinity with Israeli Jews than with American Jews. In some respects, this is not surprising. American Jews are fairly liberal and only a few decades ago some of them were putting their lives and pocketbooks on the line to support the civil rights movement in the United States. In addition, about 80 percent of American Jews who voted in the last presidential election voted for Obama.

The American religious reconstructionists also have their counterparts in Israel—members of the ultra-Orthodox Sephardic Shas Party. The rabbi-run fundamentalist Shas embraces much of Israel's working class. Its opposition comes from Tel Aviv's intelligentsia and high-tech business interests. Most American Jews have little in common with those who embrace the Shas party.

One of the reasons America is so hated in the Mideast is because of its longstanding friendship with Israel.

President Obama knows that not only in America, but also in Israel, Jews do not speak with one voice. Does Sarah Palin know this? Given a choice between her country (backing out of Mideast warfare) and her dominionist religious priorities (protecting Israel at any cost), which would she choose?

WHAT ABOUT THE WARS IN IRAQ AND AFGHANISTAN?

Some observers believe the United States has passed Sarah Palin's pro-Israel stance, and her perhaps misplaced patriotic fervor put her unashamedly behind the ongoing conflicts in Iraq and Afghanistan. She is squarely against President Obama's timetable for withdrawing troops. Indeed, when a defiant Iran is in the news, she has been quoted as saying that we should wage war with it too.

One somehow feels that she has a rather simplistic black-and-white approach to what are complex problems in the Middle East. It's as though she believes we should take on any Middle Eastern country that is Israel's enemy, which would include Syria and possibly other neighboring nations. This lends credence to her perhaps looking at this as a religious war. That would be consistent with her stated belief in the end-times scenario in which Christians take over the world to prepare for the coming of Jesus to reign for 1,000 years. There are variations to this scenario for redeeming a sinful world. One of these would have everyone but the chosen Christians burning in a lake of fire.

Allies in the Mideast and our government have never been known to come anywhere near championing a religious war. In addition, wealthy Muslim investors are involved in big business not only in the United States but globally. You can find them—as well as wealthy Asians—on the boards of many Fortune 500 companies. Big business has gone global, and its head honchos are powerbrokers. There are several disturbing elements here. One is that the United States has long-standing non-Christians who often disregard national borders. Nothing indicates that this trend can be reversed.

WHAT ABOUT RUSSIA, CHINA, AND OTHER ADVERSARIES?

From the outside looking in, it appears that United States foreign policy has been restructured around globalization and that this is an ongoing process. It is interesting to watch the United States befriending Russia and China in some cases and in other cases being their adversary. There is a lot of tightrope walking among these three superpowers. Some observers believe that the United States is at its zenith as a superpower and that China is at the beginning of its ascendancy.

Does Sarah Palin understand the dynamics of our foreign policy and know who the major players are? Is she conversant on the contributing causes and how they intersect with trade policy and nuclear disarmament? Does she know which superpower holds most of the U.S. debt?

PALIN'S EXPERIENCE WITH BUDGETS

In Alaska's fiscal year 2007 then Governor Sarah Palin oversaw the management of approximately $5.5 billion in expenditures.[6] Alaska's financial picture is unlike that of any other state. It has more income than expenditures. Yet, Alaska collects from its citizens no income tax and no sales tax. Alaska sends cash to its citizens from its huge cash reserves. In 2007, slightly over 85 percent of Alaska's tax revenue came from the oil industry. A big chunk of the rest was from the federal government.

The 2009 budget was about $9 billion; the state expected to collect as much as $11 billion in revenue.[7] There are no money worries here, all the way up and back down—from department heads up to the governor, then back down to the citizens. By contrast, other governors are constantly under pressure to make ends meet. They must decide where painful cuts are made and where money is most needed.

Here are some budget items Palin was responsible for as Alaska's governor.[8]

- $70.6 million for Fish and Game's new sport fish hatchery
- $ 2 million to upgrade Anchorage swimming pools
- $ 2 million to design and install an artificial-turf football field at an Anchorage high school
- $ 25,000 for landscaping an Anchorage grade school

The above items were all for Anchorage. There's more. The list of Anchorage projects that are underwritten by the state fills thirty pages. That's "a stack of paper so thick, you can barely get a staple through it," an Anchorage newspaper reported, noting that it was "filled with so many seven and eight-figure numbers that the eyes blur at the sight of all those zeroes."[9] The budget writers claim, "We said no to a lot of stuff."[10] There is still more: The state budget included sixty-four road projects for Anchorage. It was estimated that these would support 2,000 jobs over the next three years as the money was spent.[11]

The need for these expenditures shouldn't be questioned. The problem is that it's more of a luxury list than the majority of other states—many operating with high deficits—can afford.

There's a bit of ironic humor in the list. Organizations that didn't even ask for money were given grants. One was a very worthy charity. To Methodist Church pastors Jason and Beth Armstrong, the $5,000 the budget earmarked for their food bank was like manna from heaven.[12] They buy nonperishable food for eighteen cents a pound. "That translates to over 25,000 pounds of food," Beth Armstrong said, noting that not only do these funds help hundreds of people every month, but they also provide about a two-year food supply for the bank. Hundreds of food banks across America would be envious of such bounty.

Here are some comparison figures for Palin's $5.5 billion in expenditures during fiscal year 2007. Three of these are cities in which mayors have more burdensome budgets than Sarah Palin had as a governor.

- Chicago's budget was $6.3 billion
- New York City's budget was a ginormous $59 billion
- Los Angeles weighed in at $7 billion
- The University of California system budget was $19.5 billion

Here are the 2007 figures comparing the budgets of others states with that of Alaska.

- California's budget was 131.5 billion[13]
- The Texas budget was $ 152 billion[14]
- The New York State budget was $120.9 billion[15]

The Texas budget was thirty times that of Alaska and the California budget was twenty-six times as high.

Alaska's income and expenditures are, in dollar figures, reminiscent of those the largest states had decades ago. If we go back to 1955, the difference is mind-boggling. In 1955, the total of all state revenues was $11.2 billion.[16]

Do all these statistics add up to present Sarah Palin as a big budget cutter and efficient money manager? No, there is no incentive to cut Alaska's budget because its revenues are more than adequate to pay for the services the state provides its citizens and for the administrative cost of running the government. In effect, the Alaska governor is dealing with a budget that may be the only state budget in the country that generates a surplus year after year. This century's Alaska governors have little experience in harnessing deficit budgets.

REPUBLICAN ADMINISTRATIONS FLUNKED FISCAL CONSERVATISM

George W. Bush was a president who began his term of office with no deficit budget carryover from the previous Clinton Administration. By the end of his eight years in office, the country was operating in an extreme deficit position. In addition, the U.S. economy had already plunged into a deep disaster that rippled outward until the entire global economy was jeopardized. That the blame for this has not properly been placed on the Bush Administration is a travesty, especially since his successor, President Obama, has taken so much heat for bailing out the collapsing financial sector, even though much of that loan money has already been paid back.

Beyond the year-to-year operating budget is the enormous national debt and the interest on it. Over-the-top expenditures by the administrations of Ronald Reagan and both Bush presidents accounted for three-quarters of the size of the national debt the Obama Administration inherited. With expensive military campaigns being waged in Iraq and Afghanistan, there was little Obama could do to trim the national debt.

The truth is that three Republican administrations that claimed to stand for fiscal conservatism were not adept at implementing it.

Here is a 2006 explanation of what a billion means:

- A billion seconds ago, it was 1959
- A billion minutes ago, Jesus was alive
- A billion hours ago, our ancestors were living in the Stone Age
- A billion days ago, no creature walked the earth on two feet
- But, a billion dollars lasts only eight hours and twenty minutes at the rate the government is spending it.

THE HEALTH CARE DEBATE

The Clinton Administration made an effort to pass health care reform that would rein in the skyrocketing cost of medical care but couldn't get the enabling legislation passed. The Bush Administration took a look at health care problems in the U.S., but didn't attempt to fix it even though Medicare was paying out more money than it was taking in.

Dr. William J. Rand, a Florida ophthalmologist who was asked to review the health care plan for the Bush Administration, said the first step in turning the health care crisis around would be stopping the corporate takeover of the medical care delivery system. He advocated getting rid of for-profit managed care enterprises (HMOs). At that time Dr. Rand claimed HMOs received thirty to forty cents of every health care dollar for matching patients with doctors and hospitals.[17]

Here were some of Dr. Rand's recommendations: [18]

- Apply antitrust, monopoly, and cartel laws to medical enterprises.
- Make it illegal to enter a capitation (per head) based health care relationship.

- Make it illegal to restrict a patient's access to specified providers.
- Regulate insurance and health care companies as a utility, so there would be affordable universal coverage.
- Standardize simplified claims forms and computer interfaces used by insurance companies.
- Issue a national health card.
- Require every American to obtain health care insurance the way auto owners must have motor vehicle insurance.
- Do not make citizens entitled to free services they don't need .
- Enlist doctors in a patriotic effort to hold down unnecessary health cost expenditures.
- Empower specialty medical societies to develop guidelines for efficient care.
- Give more government support to medical research, noting that as costly diseases are eliminated the overall cost for American health care should not keep escalating.

Sometimes looking from the outside in gives a clearer perception of a multi dimensional hot-button issue in which it is easy to get fired up over some of the minor issues. Carol Finch, a British woman who writes about retirement issues, said this of the America health care system Obama wanted to fix: "I'm confused now. Or, even more than before. The British perception of part of the issues you face is:[19]

- Your health care system is currently run by one or two insurance giants that are screwing the public and greasing the palms of too many politicians to have their wrists slapped.
- Those of you that are currently able to afford health care insurance are paying over the odds because of the shonky practices of the insurers and because so many people can't afford insurance, and you basically already have to cover their costs in the premiums you pay.
- Opening up the insurance market will bring in more providers who will actually turn it into a competitive market and kick the current giants in the bottom (hence the

- misinformation and political badmouthing that they are spreading and lobbying politicians to spread).
- More entrants to market will decrease costs making it easier for those who currently pay for insurance to get it cheaper and (it would be) cheaper for those that currently can't afford it. "Surely, doing anything to break their monopoly/ influence on your health care system is an improvement," Finch concluded.[20]

When President Obama began his initiative to reform the nation's health care system it was at a crisis point. The Medicare system was headed for bankruptcy, with more money going out of Medicare than was coming in. The HMOs and insurance companies were raking in huge profits. This put the squeeze on hospitals and doctors, whose share of the health care dollar had diminished significantly. Hospitals cut staff. In some hospitals there was only one registered nurse per floor. The paperwork required of this nurse often kept him/her from patient care. Dedicated nurses were staying after hours at no pay to cope with paperwork, so they could fit into their shift the nursing care they were trained to give

Could President Obama bite the bullet and make unpopular choices? Could legislators turn a deaf ear to corporate lobbyists? Health provider profiteers were heavy contributors to political campaigns. How much opposition could they generate?

President Obama's team came up with an affordable plan that included everyone. He and his advisers invited input from all legislators. In the negotiations necessary to get the legislation passed by Congress, piece after piece of the initial health care package was bargained away. The final opposition was by partisan Republicans.

Lobbyists and corporate-financed publicity campaigns had stooped to rabble rousing, their target being an already disillusioned Republican constituency. Sarah Palin joined the fray, happily passing along misinformation about the plan she probably never read. Her main message was that the Obama health plan included "death panels." She had to know what a ludicrous charge that was.

Palin referred to the provision of a House bill requiring Medicare to pay for voluntary end-of-life counseling sessions as "downright evil" in a Facebook post, either deliberately or mistakenly misconstruing its intent. Medicare already covers hospice care and legislation passed by Congress in 1990 requires that patients be asked if they have a living will.[21] The nonpartisan group FactCheck.org, a project of the Annenberg Public Policy Center at the University of Pennsylvania, was among those refuting the claim as false.

The watered-down health care bill passed in the Senate December 24, 2009 and in the House March 21, 2010. It was a victory in that it addressed crisis issues, extends the possibility of healthcare to every American and sets a framework for even more positive and necessary changes.

The American image, however, was tainted again. The can-do Americans, who could have worked in unison to produce an amazing streamlined, high-tech, and innovative health care system that would have been the envy of the world, lost a golden opportunity. Why? Because partisan legislators caved in to lobbyists and corporate pressure and didn't care about what was good for United States citizens.

What they did sits on the edge of being unpatriotic. They didn't take the responsibility or have the moral character to point out the lies.

The aftermath of the health care legislation that passed further soiled America's reputation. Threats were made against legislators who voted for it. Some were subjected to vandalism. At least one was spat at. Some of these threats and acts of violence could be classified as domestic terrorism. Yet, elected Republicans who have sworn to uphold the Constitution were encouraging acts of violence with their incendiary language.

The John McCain-Sarah Palin team that lost the 2008 presidential election disgraced themselves and the nation. Republican standard-bearer John McCain vowed to quit governing. Sarah Palin, his former running mate, posted a "hit list" of "targeted" Democrats with an online map showing their districts marked with crosshairs of rifle sights.

Sarah calls the final health care package that was passed by Congress that "mother-of-all-unfunded mandates" and wants it repealed and replaced by what she calls "real free market patient-centered health care reform."[22]

ENVIRONMENTALISM: SAVING PLANET EARTH

Sarah Palin's love for Alaska shines through page after page of *Going Rogue*. It illuminates many of her speeches. As Alaska's former governor and a lover of the outdoors, supposedly skilled at hunting and fishing, she has seen much of the state's pristine beauty first hand.

Alaska's towering mountains, volcanic islands, glaciers, and millions of acres of uninhabited spaces were highlighted in "Sarah Palin's Alaska," an eight episode TV documentary which aired on Discovery's TLC channel. [23] Sarah, who characterizes herself as an average American and everyday mom, had this high-stakes deal arranged by the same Washington lawyer who arranged for the sale of her book to Harper Collins Publishers. The TV series was sold sight unseen. Filming has not yet begun. It has been alleged that the major networks all turned down this Sarah Palin documentary, which was touted as a nature-oriented production.[24]

Part of Sarah's magnetism is that millions of Americans think that if Sarah can get books published and TV deals locked in for her treasure chest, they can too. Unfortunately, there are not enough open spots for millions to be TV stars or high-profile authors. The searing truth is that Sarah is not like these wannabes. She is a millionaire and her beautiful lakeside home is not on Main Street.

The TV series served as a grandstand for Sarah to promote the environmental movement and saving our planet. Right? No, wrong! Sarah is not an environmentalist. She does not believe people are dangerously polluting our planet. She has repeatedly referred to what she terms the Obama Administration's "environmental extremism" and has said we cannot claim with certainty that weather changes are caused by human activities.

Why would a nature lover take this stand? Well, not every nature lover does. Sarah is echoing an almost nauseating right-wing stand. Conservative politicians don't want to clamp down on the oil and automotive industries (to name only two relevant sectors of the economy.) They don't want to impose regulations that will pare down corporate profits.

Why would Christians take this stand? Not every Christian does. This is not solely a Christian issue, but it is a religious issue. More liberal Christians, as well as Muslims and Jews, plus some middle of the roaders, believe our planet earth is a gift from a creator god and therefore we have responsibility for it. It is a question of stewardship. Good stewards take care of the gifts given them. They don't harm, damage, or destroy them.

The fundamentalist religions tend to take a narrower view. Some believe only God can take care of something as big and complex as climate. Some also believe God has already planned everything, and who are we to question it? Many believe we are at the end times and close to the apocalypse, so why bother. Still others, translating Bible passages in a literal way, see the angry God of the Old Testament. When faced with something like 9/11, the devastation of severe earthquakes or the destructive force of powerful hurricanes, they conclude that God is punishing all of us for our sins. (Interestingly, they rank these sins. As an entire population, United States residents are punished less for our marauding materialism than for tolerating homosexuality or abortions.) Conservative Republicans and fundamentalist churchgoers seem to be reluctant to take the stand of "we have met the enemy and it is us."

There is, however, one instance in which Sarah Palin met the enemy, and it was a big, big business. To her credit, Sarah stayed on the side of the people. This was the aftermath of the 1989 Exxon Valdez eleven million gallon oil spill, which contaminated 1,500 square miles of Alaska shoreline. Her reaction to this economic and social disaster is well covered in *Going Rogue*.

Fisheries closed, commercial fishing boats were hauled ashore, hundreds were homeless, and banks repossessed both fishing vessels and homes. Government at every level seemed unable to hold Exxon accountable as it refused to pay court-ordered penalties for ruining entire communities and the livelihoods of their residents. Litigation and court challenges took place for nearly two decades as some of the former fishermen reached retirement age. Sarah favored $2 billion for the victims, but in the long run Alaskans had to settle for $500 million. It was a disaster that robbed people of half of their adult earning power.

The spill happened when Todd and Sarah Palin were in the first year of their marriage and a month before the birth of their first child, a son named Track because Sarah had been a high school track star, and it was the start of the track season. Years later, as Alaska's governor, Sarah filed an amicus brief on behalf of the plaintiffs and in 2008 the U.S. Supreme Court ruled in favor of the people. Both environmentalists—who considered it a slap in the face for the victims—and Sarah Palin, were disappointed in what was considered a low settlement amount.

Sarah Palin's stance on environmental issues while she held public office in Alaska was a mix between supporting Alaskan hunters in killing the animals many Alaskans used to put food on the table and developing the economy by protecting the operations of people in the lumbering, mining, and drilling sectors of the economy. Those goals did not always mesh.[25,26,27]

Here is a list of some of Palin's environmental stands:

- Encouraged timber harvesting, mining, and oil and gas drilling "to revitalize our once-robust industries."
- Took issue with the federal government over a proposal to list Cook Inlet beluga whales as an endangered species.
- Opposed Rep. George Miller's (D-CA) bill to ban shooting of wolves from aircraft in a press release that claimed there was no aerial shooting of wolves in Alaska and also stated that the state's science-driven and abundance-based predator management program involved volunteers being permitted to use aircraft to kill some predators. (Miller's bill maintained aerial shooting of wolves was a component of moose and caribou management plans in five specific areas of Alaska.)
- Took a stand against fish farming in Alaskan waters.
- Opposed protecting salmon from mining contamination.

As governor, Palin championed Alaska's suit against the federal government. It sought to overturn the U.S. Department of the Interior's decision to list the polar bear as threatened under the Endangered Species Act. Governor Palin said, "We believe that the service's decision to list the polar bear was not based on the best scientific and commercial data available. She declared that its arguments that the polar bear is threatened by sea-ice habitat loss "are not warranted."

"I always remind people from outside our state that there's plenty of room for all Alaska's animals right next to the mashed potatoes," Sarah is quoted as saying in her book, *Going Rogue*.[28]

IMMIGRATION POLICIES AND WELFARE SPENDING

Immigration policies will be a hot button issue in the run-up to the 2012 presidential election. Americans are being vocal on both sides of the debate. As is common with emotional issues, people are being vocal at both extremes, using emotional language rather than reasoned approaches to what is indeed an important problem.

Immigration issues are so complicated that they go beyond simplistic situations, including building walls and individual states framing differing laws. Immigration has always been dealt with at the federal level because it involves citizens from around the world. Several issues need to be addressed from a legal view (Department of Justice), a security viewpoint (Department of Homeland Security), and a legislative perspective (Congress), so a unified approach to the problem can be framed. Individual problems and their solutions need to be discussed and vetted. A code has to be formed to determine who is and who isn't an illegal immigrant. Penalties and procedures should be developed.

Arizona's rush to pass its own legislation may meet immediate needs and help solve existing problems faced by the state and its citizens, but sets an undesirable precedent. Were each state to form its own immigration policy, there would be so many versions that a person's legal status could depend entirely on what state he/she is in.

It is unfortunate that undesirable jobs were treated two ways by recent presidential administrations: 1) They were farmed out to other countries, which is why you may end up talking on the phone to someone in India when you are trying to find out why your credit card bill doesn't properly list your debits and credits; 2) In the hurricane-devastated south between 2004 and 2006, federal officials turned a blind eye to the number of Mexicans (some of them illegal immigrants) that were hired to replace thousands of damaged roofs and work in other construction jobs for wages lower than the federally-defined minimum wage.

A high percent of wages earned by Mexicans goes to families back home in Mexico and therefore the American economy doesn't benefit from that spending power the way it would if a government-supported initiative would have paid minimum wage to able-bodied workers who were unemployed or on welfare.

The unemployed and people on welfare have become a new social class in America. They are filling the ranks in the Tea Party and "patriot" movements, enticed by rhetoric and promises a right-wing conservative government catering to big business interests would never honor. Certain jobs are beneath them and our nation's welfare system lets that be okay. There are rural poverty pockets across the nation in which our tax money is being doled out to fourth-generation welfare recipients, many of whom are capable of serving in the labor force.

It would be encouraging if someone in the White House Office of Budget and Management would try to find out why our government seemingly thinks it profitable to pay welfare to able-bodied workers at the same time our nation does nothing pertinent to keep illegal immigrants from working at the lower end of the job market. There must be a point at which outsourcing jobs and letting illegal Mexicans work in this country becomes unprofitable for a government paying out hundreds of millions of dollars to people on welfare. Indeed, it might be cheaper for the U.S. government to give a few billion dollars to Mexico to use to stimulate jobs within its own economy.

The total fiscal year 2000 cost of seventy welfare programs overseen by six federal government departments (71.6 percent), plus welfare programs funded by state and local welfare programs (28.4 percent), totaled $434.3 billion, according to the Heritage Foundation, which describes itself as "a research and educational institution—a think tank—whose mission is to formulate and promote conservative public policies based on the principles of free enterprise, limited government, individual freedom, traditional American values, and a strong national defense."[29]

According to the Heritage Foundation, between 1981, when Ronald Reagan became president, and 2000, the cost of welfare doubled. The only significant welfare reform during this period was enacted in 1996 during the Clinton Administration. According to the Heritage Foundation it dramatically cut caseloads, financial outlays, and food stamp enrollments. No definitive figures are available for the last decade but probably will be after the 2010 census is tabulated. Because of the global financial crisis and the rate of home foreclosures in the United States during the past two years, the amount of money spent on welfare is probably past the half-a-trillion dollar mark.

Where is Palin on this hot-button issue?

When asked in 2006 about Alaska's growth surge in minority and immigration populations, Palin, then a gubernatorial candidate, said, "I have reached out to all these communities and asked them to identify their needs. Their response has been for more vocational training, seniors' assistance, ending gang violence, and more state outreach and communication with their communities." [30] Sarah said that it was not humane, nor economically feasible, to round up and deport about twelve million illegal immigrants. That was from a 2008 interview by Jorge Ramos for Univision. In the same interview she said she did not support amnesty for all undocumented immigrants and noted that those who are in the country legally should be first in line for job opportunities and government-provided services. Palin said then that she also supported a path to citizenship for illegal immigrants because she understands why people want to be in America, the land of opportunity. When Sarah Palin resigned as Alaska's governor, she appeared to have a much more lenient approach to illegal immigration than members of the perceived constituency she has been building between then and now.

Palin did not initially endorse Arizona's new immigration legislation but finally signed on to the Arizona bandwagon, giving support to Arizona governor Jan Brewer. "It's time for Americans across this great country to stand up and say 'We're all Arizonans now and, in clear unity, we say, 'Mr. President, do your job, secure our border,'" Palin said at a May 15, 2010 press conference with Governor Brewer in Phoenix. This appears to be a political about-face.

Palin did not hold up well under Bill O'Reilly's grilling about immigration reform on his July 9, 2010 Fox News show. After Palin indicated she didn't want to talk about the details of immigration reform, he kept trying to get her to explain how she would handle the nuts and bolts of dealing with twelve million immigrants. No go. Sarah had nothing to reveal. By the show's end even O'Reilly looked a bit taken aback by her evasiveness and nonanswers.

PALIN ON WELFARE REFORM

Where is Sarah Palin on welfare reform? She is very supportive of the earned income tax credit (EITC). The EITC is a refundable federal income tax credit that targets people who work but earn low wages. It is a work-support program, designed to encourage employment for those people who would otherwise be on welfare. It provides a financial incentive to work and permits low-income workers to keep more of the money they earn. While serving as Alaska's governor, Palin signed a proclamation declaring February 1, 2008, as Alaska Earned Income Tax Credit Awareness Day, and urged eligible Alaskans to apply for the EITC. Other than that, Sarah has had little to say about government welfare reform, but there is some reading between the lines to be done.

Another Palin proclamation praised the work of the Salvation Army, which she referred to as "an evangelical part of the universal Christian Church and its mission is to preach the gospel of Jesus Christ and to meet human needs in his name without discrimination." This proclamation declared November 15, 2007 as Red Kettle Day in Alaska and encouraged citizens to give to local charities. This and other Palin statements indicate that she may envision a future in which the federal government will not help the poor but instead local or regional charities, many of them probably faith-based initiatives, would provide for the needs of the poor.

THE ABORTION ISSUE

It often seems that Sarah's religious zeal has as its two-themed centerpiece her antiabortion position and her crusade for "family values" that need to be further explained. Family values will probably be a major topic in her upcoming book. Her ability to galvanize those "mama grizzlies" into action rests squarely on those themes.

There is an almost surreal quality about the opening scene of *Going Rogue*. There she is at the Alaska State Fair, baby Trig in her arms and Piper, seven, tagging along. It is a world of cotton candy and proudly displayed homegrown giant vegetables, of craft displays and livestock competitions, of squealing kids on rides, and of blaring music as a local dance troupe takes the stage.

Sarah calls Piper "my constant sidekick since the moment she was born." Then Sarah sees the Alaska Right to Life booth where, in her words, a poster catches her eye and takes her breath away. The poster features "the sweetest baby girl swathed in pink pretend angel wings." Next: "That's you, baby," she whispers to Piper, telling the reader "as I have every year." The reader is then told that Sarah thinks it is a nice shot, as she notes every time she see it on an ad or fund-raiser ticket.

In a nutshell, Sarah is prolife and wants to see that every baby that is created lives to have a future and potential. She believes legislators should do everything possible to protect human life

Sarah Palin was asked for her views on abortion by the Eagle Forum in a July of 2006 questionnaire for Alaska's gubernatorial candidates, and she replied, "I am prolife with the exception of a doctor's determination that the mother's life would end if the pregnancy continued. I believe that no matter what mistakes we make as a society, we cannot condone ending another life." Earlier in the campaign, Palin had said that no woman should have to choose between her education, career, and her child, explaining that she is for the use of contraceptives and that she was a member of a prowoman but antiabortion group called Feminists for Life. "I believe in the strength and the power of women and the potential of every human life," Palin said.[31]

Later in the Alaska gubernatorial campaign Sarah was asked to what extent abortion should be prohibited in Alaska if *Roe* v. *Wade* was overturned. She wisely noted that it would not be up to the governor to ban anything and added, "It would be up to the people of Alaska to discuss and decide how we would like our society to reflect our values." She also noted that she did not approve of the use of public funds for elective abortions.[32]

While Sarah was Alaska governor the state passed its Safe Haven for Infants Act to cope with abandonment of infants. The bill lets a parent safely surrender a newborn child without threat of prosecution on the condition that there is no evidence that the infant has been physically injured. Without penalty, a parent may leave the infant in the custody of a peace officer, doctor, hospital employee, emergency medical service worker or volunteer, or employee of a fire station.

"All children deserve to begin their lives in a loving, protective family," Governor Palin said. "When that fails, it is our job as a state to make sure that children are protected."[33] Another initiative of her administration was to seek adoptions for foster care children as a more permanent setting for their safe growth, development and nurturing. This was described in her October 22, 2007 proclamation naming November 2007 as Adoption Awareness Month in Alaska.

Sarah's stand on abortion is not radical. As far as prolifers go, she can be considered a middle-of-the-road adherent. As long as she does not advocate state or federal governments mandating anti-abortion regulations—and therefore interfering in the private life of an individual—her position is a tenable one. However, when we look at abortion-related issues, there is some indication that Palin might push for such government intervention.

When it comes to rape, Alaska has the worst record of any state. The Alaskan rape rate is two and one-half times the national average. Democrat Eric Croft, a former state representative, sponsored a state law requiring Alaska cities to provide free examinations to rape victims. He said the only resistance he met was from Wasilla, where Sarah Palin was mayor from 1996 to 2002. "It was one of those things everyone could agree on except for Wasilla," Croft said. "We couldn't convince the chief of police to stop charging them." In 2000 the Alaska Legislature banned the practice of charging women for rape exam kits, which experts said could cost up to $1,000. Some Palin supporters claimed she didn't know about the Wasilla practice of charging for rape kits, but critics said this was outrageous and have questioned Palin's commitment to helping women who are the victims of violence.[34]

Sarah Palin said that if her own daughter were raped, she would choose life. The remark was made on a public TV debate four days before Palin became Alaska's youngest governor at age forty-two.

Palin is also on record as opposing stem cell research and physician-assisted suicide.

Where Palin, as an elected official, might be most inclined to urge governmental action on prohibiting abortion is by making it one of many states' rights issues. Some of her remarks about abortion lean in that direction. In considering that framework, it is appropriate to give some background.

The United States current abortion policy is rooted in the 1973 Supreme Court decision in *Roe* v. *Wade*. It legalized abortion, basing it on a Constitutional provision that supports every citizen's right to individual privacy. This gives every woman the right to choice when it comes to having an abortion. The court ruling gave rise to a pro-choice position for abortion defenders and a pro-life position for anti-abortionists.

Palin's prolife advocacy is probably bolstered by a belief that in *Roe v. Wade* the judges were making law rather than interpreting it. If she feels strongly about this, she could be viewed as believing in strict constructionism. This refers to a literal interpretation of the Constitution (with no implied rights). In a joined-at-the-hip analogy, this literal interpretation of the Constitution is the same approach many members of fundamentalist religious denominations—Sarah Palin being one of them—take to interpreting the Bible. If the Bible says so, it has to be true. Taken to the extreme, you can bait a fundamentalist by declaring that the Bible makes it clear that adulterous women are to be stoned to death, but that in the United States societal and cultural moral customs, as well as, our laws, do not permit the stoning to death of such women.

Antiabortion legislators from time to time introduce "human life bills" in Congress. Most of this legislation seeks to overturn *Roe v. Wade*, which means returning decision making about abortion to the states. It would not ban abortion. Others want a Human Life Amendment to the Constitution that would ban abortion in all states.

Taken to extremes, States Rights activism, which is a mindset that embraces several issues, could result in a United States as polarized as it was at the advent of the Civil War. People with conservative politics and fundamentalist religion would flock to some states, and people from the mainstream Christian religions, as well as people from other major religions and those with no religion, would flock to other states. States would then either become conservative, leaning toward fascism, or be liberal, leaning toward socialism. (Communism does not, by its nature, play any definitive role in this scenario.)

Many Americans, reacting to recent vitriolic language, ugly name-calling and threats, including Sarah Palin's 2010 "We need a revolution" speech to the Tea Party Convention and the growth of antigovernment militia units, fear this sort of showdown. They wonder if America would continue to be a democracy, thereby guaranteeing the freedom that people in many countries are denied?

An unpredictable Palin mixed politics, petty grievances with the press, her antiabortion crusading and a seemingly uneducated understanding of the Constitutional role of a free press, into a screwed up stew in April 2010.

Palin was appearing at an Austin, Texas, fund-raiser by Heroic Media, a group that tries to reduce the number of abortions through media outreach. Speaker Sarah Palin was probably paid a caviar-level speaking fee. In order to cover the event, however, members of the media had to buy a $50 ticket, with proceeds to benefit Heroic Media (probably paying Sarah's speaking fee). Sarah must not have understood the game plan. What a way to sabotage an organization's "media outreach" project![35]

ALL THE OTHER ISSUES:

The best way to see how Sarah feels about various other issues is to read her own words. Dozens of actual Sarah Palin quotations on such things as homeland security, war and peace, free trade, energy and oil, gun control, crime, drugs, jobs, government reform, tax reform, social security, technology, education, and corporations can be found at the On the Issues Web site (www.ontheissues.org/Sarah Palin.htm). Sources are given for these authentic quotations. These quotes, however, only establish a baseline that dates from the 2008 presidential race.

CHAPTER POSTSCRIPT

Persons interested in continuing to track Palin's views can keep current by reading newspapers that have nationwide circulation such as *Today* and the *New York Times*. The *Washington Post*, which offers in-depth political analysis, is also helpful. The news-centered magazines, such as *Time*, *Newsweek,* and *U.S. News and World Report*, are informative. For an outsider's perspective of U.S. politics, England's the *Guardian* is an excellent source.

Many of these mainstream sources are accessible online. Avoid hate-oriented Web sites. When rumors run rampant on the Web you can check their authenticity at Web sites that specialize in proving or disproving Internet rumors, scams, hoaxes, and other types of misinformation. Just enter into your browser a couple of words describing what you want checked and put either before or after them the term *fact-check*. There is also a Web site that keeps a running tally of President Obama's campaign promises, noting whether he has kept them, compromised on them, or broken them. It also notes for more than 300 Obama promises how many are stalled or "in the works."

CHAPTER FOUR

SARAH PALIN'S POLITICS: A NEW WORLD RECIPE?

"Most economic fallacies derive from the tendency to assume that there is a fixed pie, that one party can gain only at the expense of another."
~ Milton Friedman

Sarah Palin repeatedly refers to her own position as being a rogue and individualist who is far from being a team player. In her first days as a member of Wasilla's town council, members had to decide whether or not people living in new subdivisions should pay for weekly trash removal, instead of transporting their own garbage to the dump, as the Palins did. This was the first of many difficult decisions Sarah would have to make around politics-as-usual issues. The councilman who had invited her to run for this office turned out to be a beneficiary of the proposed pay-for-garbage-removal issue. He owned the town's garbage truck company. It is this type of encounter that makes politics such an unattractive work arena.

Sarah voted against the proposal, explaining in *Going Rogue* that she voted according to her principles and let the chips fall where they may.[1] That is admirable. The postscript, however, is what happens when this self-professed rugged individualist and sometimes loose cannon votes according to her principles and is way off the mark of what members of her constituency desire?

IDEOLOGY

Remember the murder-suicide rampage of Andrew Joseph Stack III? He's the angry tax protester who rammed a plane into an Austin,

Texas, Internal Revenue Service building February 18, 2010. It was an event *New York Times* columnist Frank Rich labeled as a flare with the dark afterlife of an omen.[2] What did he mean? Rich explains what made that kamikaze mission eventful was less the deranged act itself than the curious reaction of politicians on the right who gave it a pass or, worse, flirted with condoning it. Stack left a political legacy in the form of a written rant condemning the IRS and the government. Like-minded people were soon building shrines to him on Facebook. A couple of decades ago they would have been called kooks.

It's unbelievable how times have changed so swiftly. The incident spread its antigovernment tentacles even wider. Some Republican politicians were letting their constituency know they empathized with Stack. They sympathized with his motives, not his actions. It is hard to decide which is most outrageous: that Rep. Steve King of Iowa called the IRS an unnecessary agency, or that fellow legislators didn't fall all over themselves trying to rein him in after he said that when we abolish the IRS, it's going to be a happy day for America. If King doesn't feel the IRS provides a necessary function, why depend on suicidal murderers to get the message out? He's a legislator, and legislators have a role most of us don't. They can change things. One is tempted to muse a bit about Congressman King wanting the IRS abolished. Does that mean he wants to do away with taxation? Does he want to serve without pay? What alternative fund-raisers does he suggest?

This calls to mind Sarah Palin's constant blanket statement that the folks in Washington don't do a good job, are not knowledgeable about local affairs, and are not necessary to the functioning of our country. Yet, she has not outlined another system for us to operate under and remain a democracy. So, if these people had their way would we have no federal government? Would that be the end of democracy as we know it? After all, our government functions by the people electing officials to go to Washington to act on our behalf.

Americans need to know what are the real goals and purposes of these antigovernment people. Some say the Tea Partiers want to abolish most government agencies and do away with entitlement programs. Well, if they bitched because registration fees for the first Tea Party convention were too high and if they didn't like the cost of Sarah Palin's speaking engagement there, then how are they going to find the money for medical and nursing home care during their retirement? Perhaps they should start building rooms onto their homes because, if they think these changes are coming soon, they best be prepared to support any relatives who are on welfare. They may have to pay for their parents to be in nursing homes, also foot their medical bills and pay for their prescriptions.

Without Social Security, which is one of the big three entitlement programs, many of their parents won't even have change to pay for toiletries, food, clothes, or a bottle of booze. Columnist Frank Rich believes the Palin/Tea Party leadership has a firm and dangerous ideology that plays to the "lock-and-load nut cases" out there, not just to the peaceable (if riled up) populist conservatives attracted to Tea Partyism.[4]

People over sixty will recall the John Birch Society, a far-right group from the 1960s. Look closely. The Birchers are coming out of hibernation. Like-minded groups are sprouting on the tree whose branches wave to the right-oriented wind. Beware of the Oath Keepers. This militia of veterans and ex-law enforcement types champions breaking laws you don't believe in. Are you sure, Sarah, that you want to play ball with these folks? Sounds like they might cheat on the game rules.

THREE POLITICAL MOVEMENTS

There are three political movements trying to work their way into the U.S. mainstream. They are:

1. The New World Order, composed of powerful interrelated giant global enterprises.
2. The Tea Party movement, which currently is fragmented but could coalesce enough to gain high leadership positions in American government. Tea Partiers want to dismantle federal government and transfer more power to individual states.
3. A populist movement that does not want to dismantle government but instead clean it up, stabilize it, and make it truly responsive to its citizens by taking power away from the moneyed interests.

All the right-wing talk about socialism is a scare tactic. At present, there is no organized movement to base our government upon the precepts of socialism. Were there would-be politicians leaning in that direction, they would have formed a viable Socialist Party as an option to the Democrats or Republicans. That is what they have done in England, France, and other countries.

There is no widespread public knowledge about any of the three movements cited above, although the Tea Party has been getting large press coverage, probably because they are the new kid on the block.

The majority of American citizens appear to think they are still living in the traditional two-party system and could easily awake on the eve of the next presidential election to discover this is no longer true. The burden of making it so, however, means these three movements must define themselves, their goals, and how they intend to reach them. This means they might not get their act together soon enough to fill the White House or gain majority status in the Congress in 2012.

What about the Democrats? Americans who wanted a change—and supported the Obama candidacy—do not think they are getting that change. The extent to which Obama is able to disempower, or regulate, financial networks can be translated into cues for the three movements.

If the Obama Administration is unable to rein in the power of financial empires, that is a signal that the New World Order folks have a lot of clout behind the scenes. It also might signify that the Tea Party movement would need the biblical David to slay the financial Goliath. Because the New World Order and the Tea Party movements are both fueled by Republicans, the Democrats might have an uphill battle to wrest votes away from a combined Republican/Tea Party. It might make sense for them to adopt the populist platform.

Where does Sarah Palin fit in? She appears to have connections with both the architects of the New World Order and those of the Tea Party movement. Both do include conservative Republicans. The fact that she has lent support, including donations from her war chest, to a few fairly moderate Republicans indicates that if, indeed, she aspires to national leadership, she or her behind-the-scenes handlers are shrewdly watching how things unfold.

THE NEW WORLD ORDER

The New World Order resurrects a decades-old concept in which Karl Rove, Donald Rumsfeld, Dick Cheney, Richard Perle, and Paul Wolfowitz were major players. It is seen as a move toward globalization facilitated by a network of international banking gurus, a few select international organizations, and both the American military defense industry and corporate giants whose business already transcends national boundaries. These powers, it is suggested, yield much more clout than heads of government.

The term *new world order* has been used in the past to describe many movements, most of which either fizzled out, or were conspiracy theories. Here in America in 2010 the context of new world order is a specific political platform whose architects—Rumsfeld, Cheney, Perle, Wolfowitz, and others—were tied to the administration of the first President Bush.

Behind the scenes, these men held conferences with like-minded individuals, set agendas, and goals, and were working toward globalization. They envisioned a world run in the interests of people of wealth and/or power. They went so far as to plan propaganda campaigns that described this new world order as creating global peace (after the United States first fought wars to spread democracy in such places as the Mid East).

Some of these same players turned up in the highest positions in the administration of the second Bush president, an administration that insisted it was trying to bring democracy, peace and prosperity to Iraq and Afghanistan when the objectives were really to harness and control vast natural gas and oil reserves needed to feed the New World Order's money-making machine.

THE EISENHOWER WARNING

President Dwight Eisenhower had a military background. As a leader familiar with the military and with politics, he had a warning for future Americans. First, however, his background. Eisenhower was a five-star general who served as supreme commander of the allied forces in Europe during World War II and in 1951 became first supreme commander of NATO. He won the 1952 presidential race by a landslide.

Eisenhower is often portrayed as a benevolent man and a humanist, which he was. He had also earned a lot of credibility and trust. Yet, he had a feisty foreign policy and forced China to agree to a cease fire in the Korean War by threatening the use of nuclear weapons.

When the Soviets launched the Sputnik satellite in 1957, he doggedly pursued the goal of America catching up in the space race. He also enlarged the Social Security program and launched the interstate highway system. It was in his administration that Hawaii (later the birthplace of Barack Obama) and Alaska (home of Sarah Palin) were admitted to statehood.

Although historians often rank Eisenhower among the top ten presidents, Republican politicians of recent decades rarely cite him as an example, even though his eight years in office were, overall, marked by peace and prosperity. There is a reason for this. Eisenhower gave his televised farewell speech to the nation January 17, 1961. In it, citing the Cold War, he characterized the Soviets as having a hostile ideology, atheistic character, and insidious methods.

Eisenhower was concerned about unjustified government spending proposals and warned that we must guard against the acquisition of unwarranted influence, whether sought or unsought, by the military-industrial complex; he said that the potential for the disastrous rise of misplaced power exists and will persist. He noted that only an alert and knowledgeable citizenry could compel the proper meshing of the huge industrial and military machinery of defense with our peaceful methods and goals, so that security and liberty may prosper together.

PEOPLE WEARING MANY HATS

The military-industrial complex players have rather intricate relationships between the executive and legislative branches of the government, the Department of Defense and all the subcontractors that produce armaments. These relationships become questionable when roles of policymakers are not clearly defined and power and control issues have a negative impact on decision making.

An example: Dick Cheney, vice president for the second Bush president, had been secretary of defense during the first Bush presidency. While out of government office, Cheney served as chairman and CEO of Halliburton Company from 1995 to 2000. Halliburton, one of the world's largest oilfield services corporations, operates in more than seventy countries, has dozens of subsidiaries, affiliates, branches, and divisions worldwide, and employs over 50,000 people.[5,6] Halliburton, previously headquartered in Houston, has relocated its corporate offices to Dubai in the United Arab Emirates.[7] As vice president, Cheney was a prominent member of the National Energy Policy Development Group (NEPDG), also called the energy task force, which included energy industry representatives. (This is not to imply any wrongdoing on Cheney's part, but only to note the interrelationships of political power, the energy sector interests and military contracts with the corporate defense industry.)

President Eisenhower foresaw dangerous complications arising from the arena in which political approval is given for all stages of military hardware and accompanying accoutrements. It is a world in which government officials and private corporations negotiate lucrative contracts for research, development, production, use, and support not only for military training but also for warfare use. In addition to covering weapons and equipment, it includes facilities and the furnishing and supplying of them.

WHAT EISENHOWER WITNESSED

Eisenhower had seen firsthand the quick advances of technology and how they applied to warfare. He watched the almost overnight growth of the companies with products and services in this sector. Then it was becoming a multimillion dollar operation. Now it is a multibillion dollar operation. To put it bluntly, he foresaw that a lot of people in high government offices and their corporate counterparts could decide to wage war because it was lucrative. This, he thought, would be an immoral war for war's sake.

This network of contacts and contracts, of money and resources, is always ripe for corruption because so much of the jockeying is done out of the public eye. And so it is that an entity such as Halliburton can win government contracts worth billions and, unchecked, waste millions of dollars in constructing and supplying military facilities in Iraq.

There are also more sinister outgrowths of this system. The government can hire mercenary soldiers to do undercover work or handle assignments that dare not be entrusted to the U.S. military, since the military is accountable to the public. An example is Blackwater, which was indicted for illegal activities in Iraq. Blackwater ostensibly was hired to provide security services. They did that and more. Many of their highly trained mercenary soldiers are former members of the marine special forces who worked closely with the CIA. Blackwater paramilitary employees were able to conduct missions in Iraq that were considered too sensitive to entrust to the U.S. military. There is a shroud of secrecy around many of their missions.

What Eisenhower failed to predict was how international this tangled web could grow. An example is the RAND Corporation, which holds several government contracts to provide think tank services (i.e., advice on policy making) to numerous clients, among them the U.S. Department of Defense and other agencies of the U.S. government. He would have been appalled—and we should be too—to discover that members of foreign governments have served as directors and/or advisory board members of RAND.

Eisenhower also was not aware of how some of the U.S. defense contractors would become multinational companies, with foreigners on their boards. He also had no way of knowing that the scope of this military industrial complex could cover so much of the globe and have so much impact on worldwide financial networks. The tentacles reach so far that it is not much of a leap of the imagination to believe there is every reason an international network of powerful individuals could run—make that rule—the world. That could mean that a country's elected presidents and other officials are not where the buck stops, in terms of both spending money and decision-making.

There is perspective. If governments cannot live in peace with each other, perhaps business leaders can. They now have the advantage of operating in multiple countries and, often, multiple cultures with people of varying religious backgrounds. The question remains—does money talk louder than guns?

CROSS POLLINATION: BUSINESS AND GOVERNMENT

The Carlyle Group is an interesting example of cross-pollination. It is global. It has had not only former Republican U.S. officials on its board but also top ranking former U.S. Democrats as well. This indicates that, when it comes to operating on a global scale, party politics don't matter. The extension of this is that our government may not matter. It may be co-opted.

According to its Web site, the Carlyle Group is a global private equity investment firm based in Washington, D.C., with more than $88.6 billion of equity capital in sixty-seven funds under management. More than 400 investment professionals operate out of offices in nineteen countries. Both the Bush and bin Laden families were among its investors when the 9/11 onslaught on the New York World Trade Center towers took place. George H.W. Bush, father of the country's president at the time, was a senior adviser to the Carlyle Group.

Frank Charles Carlucci typifies how well some of Carlyle's leaders are plugged in. His government career included leadership positions in the U.S. Foreign Service, the Central Intelligence Agency, the Office of Management and Budget, the Department of Health, Education, and Welfare, and the Office of Economic Opportunity. He was also President Reagan's National Security Advisor and U.S. Secretary of Defense from 1987 until 1989. Carlucci is chairman emeritus of the Carlyle Group and is a director of United Defense Industries, the largest U.S. defense contractor, which is owned by the Carlyle Group. He is also a trustee of the RAND Corporation and cochair of its Center for Middle East Public Policy, as well as, a member of the Project for the New American Century, which states one of its objectives is "to rally support for a vigorous and principled policy of American international involvement."

So, how much clout does the military industrial complex have? Here's what journalist Seymour Hersh had to say about military influence on President Barack Obama at The sixth Global Conference of Investigative Journalism, in Geneva: "the military are dominating him on the important issues of the world: Iraq, Iran, Afghan and Pakistan. And he's following the policies of Bush and Cheney almost to a fare-thee-well. He talks differently. And he's much brighter, he's much more of the world. So one only hopes he has a game plan that will include doing something."[8]

There are aspects of the New World Order that are attractive, if only its proponents had as their aim improving the world instead of acquiring power and wealth. Global peace, good standards of living for everyone, an end to poverty everywhere on planet earth, adequate education, and health care for everyone, and benefits that, among other things, mean nobody has to lose their life savings because they are ill—how wonderful that would be!

What a wonderful world! This may be an attainable goal. There is, however, a disconnect. If this world would be so wonderful for all its inhabitants, then why would not its present proponents be telling us about it and asking for our support? If this became our reality, it would be like a dream come true. It would be us building heaven on earth for our Creator.

One suspects that we are not told about it because the architects of this heaven on earth would really be presenting something imperfect. It would be heaven for the rich and powerful who planned it, made it happen, and would reap the benefits. For the rest of us it would be, way before the twenty-second century, a start down the road to hell.

THE TEA PARTY MOVEMENT

The timing of the Tea Party movement is interesting. The Republican Party establishment we recognize from past decades is falling into disarray. Its conservative right wing has sucked the power out of a party that once had a cadre of strong middle-of-the-road leaders, with some liberals and some conservatives.

It is ironic that what is now closest to what the Republican Party used to be is the Democratic Party!

The Tea Partiers, however, make strange bedfellows for the right-wingers. The Tea Party movement portrays itself as a populist grass-roots movement whereas Republicans have long depended upon the deep pockets of wealthy financiers, industrialists, and corporate board members.

Sarah Palin often aligns herself with Tea Partiers, but some of her more radical following within the self-styled patriot movement and its allied militias might not be welcomed by Tea Party standard bearers.

THE "CONTRACT FROM AMERICA"

The Tea Party movement has come up with a ten-point Contract from America that they want Congress to follow. It was spearheaded by Ryan Hecker, a conservative activist who said the grass-roots movement he is identified with wants to restructure our relationship with elected officials.

It was not made clear if this is the movement's basic document or whether they will come up with others that relate to the executive and judicial branches of the government.[9] Hecker, a 2005 Harvard Law School graduate, is with Vinson & Elkins, a Texas law firm offering a range of legal services to global businesses through a network of 750 lawyers working in fourteen offices around the globe. There are offices in the Middle East, as well as in China, Japan, Russia, London, New York, and Washington.[10] According to the firm's Web site, its original partners cut their teeth on oil and gas matters, and today it remains one of the world's leading energy law firms. It really sounds like it should be aligned with the New World Order.

Hecker reports that the Contract from America was produced using an online voting process. It was officially unveiled during an April 15, 2010 Tax Day rally at the Washington Monument. Listed below are its ten agenda items. Included is a figure that reportedly is the percentage of the vote each item received in online balloting. [11]

1. Protect the Constitution: Require each bill to identify the specific provision of the Constitution that gives Congress the power to do what the bill does (82.03 percent).
2. Reject Cap and Trade: Stop costly new regulations that would increase unemployment, raise consumers' prices, and weaken the nation's global competitiveness with virtually no impact on global temperatures (72.20 percent).
3. Demand a Balanced Budget: Begin the Constitutional amendment process to require a balanced budget with a two-thirds majority needed for any tax hike. (69.69 percent)
4. Enact Fundamental Tax Reform: Adopt a simple and fair single-rate tax system by scrapping the internal revenue code and replacing it with one that is no longer than 4,543

words— the length of the original Constitution. (64.90 percent).

5. Restore Fiscal Responsibility and Constitutionally Limited Government in Washington: Create a blue ribbon task-force that engages in a complete audit of federal agencies and programs, assessing their constitutionality and identifying duplication, waste, or ineffectiveness; it would also note agencies and programs better left to state or local authorities or that are ripe for wholesale reform or elimination because of our efforts to restore limited government consistent with the U.S. Constitution's meaning. (63.37 percent)

6. End Runaway Government Spending: Impose a statutory cap limiting the annual growth in total federal spending to the sum of the inflation rate plus the percentage of population growth. (56.57 percent).

7. Defund, Repeal, and Replace Government-run Health Care: Defund, repeal, and replace the recently passed government-run health care with a system that actually makes health care and insurance more affordable by enabling a competitive, open, and transparent free-market health care and health insurance system that isn't restricted by state boundaries. (56.39 percent).

8. Pass an 'All-of-the-Above' Energy Policy: Authorize the exploration of proven energy reserves to reduce our dependence on foreign energy sources from unstable countries and reduce regulatory barriers to all other forms of energy creation, lowering prices and creating competition and jobs. (55.51 percent).

9. Stop the Pork: Place a moratorium on all earmarks until the budget is balanced, and then require a two-thirds majority to pass any earmark. (55.47 percent).

10. Stop the Tax Hikes: Permanently repeal all tax hikes, including those to the income, capital gains, and death taxes, currently scheduled to begin in 2011. (53.38 percent).

Hecker claims he began with about 1,000 submitted ideas, pared the list down to about fifty of the most popular ones and, with the help of former House Republican leader Dick Armey, arrived at the final ten. It was Armey's group, FreedomWorks, that sponsored the April 15 rally.[12]

This 2010 document was, Hecker told ABC News, inspired by Newt Gingrich's 1994 Contract for America and has Gingrich's backing. The preamble to this Contract from America states that it is based on the principles of individual liberty, limited government, and economic freedom.[13]

HOW WOULD THIS "CONTRACT" WORK?

Here are questions for Americans to ponder:
- Does this individual liberty apply to homosexuals, Muslims, and, indeed, to all humanity?
- If limited government means transferring numerous federal agencies and their programs to the state level, can Americans expect every state to then have a state income tax roughly equal to 20 percent to 25 percent of all of an individual's income?
- How will lightly populated states such as the Dakotas, Vermont, and Rhode Island be able to finance programs to provide welfare to the poor, health services, and pensions to retired persons, or unemployment benefits to laid-off workers?
- Has anyone thought all this through?
- What is this economic freedom? Does it mean the government no longer regulates American businesses?
- Does it mean restraints on certain businesses practices that keep corporations from being too greedy will be removed?

There is a strange dichotomy here. We have a contract put together by someone who earns his living in a firm that helps big businesses. Analyze this overview by Vinson and Elkins Managing Partner Joseph C. Dilg: "For almost a century, Vinson & Elkins lawyers have provided innovative business solutions for clients whose needs are as diverse as the entities they represent. In today's challenging environment of global markets, volatile economies and complex human and environmental issues, our time-tested role as trusted advisor has become even more critical."[14] He says the firm serves clients from start-up, to the negotiating table and boardroom, before legislative and regulatory bodies, in the courtroom, and beyond.

Sarah Palin, of course, has been making "drill, baby, drill" speeches for years. Oil revenue is Alaska's lifeline. Within a week of the huge BP oil platform disaster that for months spurted millions of gallons of oil into the Gulf of Mexico, Sarah spoke out on the need for continued oil drilling there.

OIL, TEA PARTY CONTRACT, AND PALIN SUPPORTERS

There is something that doesn't wash clean here, and it's a billions-of-dollars distinction. How does the clothesline reach from Hecker's compact to Sarah Palin's supporters—the Wal-Mart and hockey moms, the mama grizzlies, and all those Joe six-packs?

One perspective is that there can be no direct line between them. Who benefits from chopping down the size of the federal government? The key is in lawyer Dilg's statement. His firm represents clients before legislative and regulatory bodies. America's biggest businesses and corporate giants with worldwide reach want the federal government's regulatory bodies eliminated. They want economic freedom to do as they please. They don't like having to comply with environmental regulations like the Clean Air Act that cost them money. The drug companies don't want the Food and Drug Administration telling them how much and what kind of testing they must do before being allowed to market new products. Food manufacturers don't want inspectors showing up to test cleanliness in their processing facilities. It's a long list.

Before Tea Partiers and Palin supporters jump on the conservative Republican bandwagon they need to consider that these regulatory agencies exist to protect them and all American citizens. They are checking how polluted the air we breathe is, how many preservatives are in the food we eat, and whether toxic chemicals are leaching into our soil and poisoning the cows that provide our milk and the pigs and steers whose meat we eat. They are trying to find cures for diseases and warn us of health hazards and epidemics. They determine if work places are safe.

Many of Sarah's supporters know nothing about regulating bodies and how they operate. They don't know that these federal agencies often keep big business from ripping off America's ordinary people.

We need these agencies on the federal level, not in separate watered-down state agencies. The cost of building and staffing fifty such agencies for the separate states far surpasses the cost of having one centralized facility.

IS SARAH PALIN STRADDLING A PRICKLY POLICY FENCE?

The Tea Party movement is like a giant umbrella organization that is trying to round up different factions of American society, ostensibly to give them a voice. That voice will end up being the voice of its leaders.

Where is Sarah Palin in all of this? If she ends up on a picket fence with one leg on the New World Order side and the other on the Tea Party side, it will become so uncomfortable she will have to dismount. Either Sarah knows exactly what is going on and is laughing all the way to the bank, or she is politically naïve and being taken advantage of as a newly arrived celebrity icon that has shown success in rallying ordinary Americans.

For some reason, millions of Americans either cannot or do not want to seriously consider the power plays going on. If the Tea Party activists want to get serious, they could take all of that angry energy most Americans have and use it to tackle all of the congressmen, regardless of party, who remain aligned with the well-heeled Wall Street lobbyists, the banks fearful of new federal regulations, the insurance industry giants whose lobbying resulted in a watered-down health care reform bill, and the rich energy sector that has so many friends in Washington that it can deliberately ignore regulations designed to have oil drillers operate more safely.

These are the big money interests that have traditionally had Republican Party support. They are the culprits for outsourcing jobs overseas, doing away with much of the middle class, turning the shoulder on poverty in America, and keeping Main Street's small family businesses from accessing the capital they need to compete in the twenty-first century.

RAND PAUL SAYS PROBLEMS CROSS PARTY LINES

The Tea Party Contract does have some commonsense provisions. They are changes that also appeal to many Democrats and members of their constituency. Earlier on the day Rand Paul wrested the Kentucky Republican Party primary vote from Trey Grayson, he joined CBS News Senior White House Correspondent Bill Plante on Tuesday's *Washington Unplugged* and explained this isn't an issue of Republican versus Democrat but a referendum on the out-of-control spending endorsed by both parties in Washington.[15]

Paul's opponent was backed by some of the most powerful Republicans in Washington, including former vice president Dick Cheney and Senate minority leader Mitch McConnell (R-KY), who had handpicked Grayson.

"Neither party has controlled the debt very well and neither party has controlled spending," Paul said. "So I think the Tea Party is about bringing government back to its senses and a lot of the things we talk about are a chastisement to both parties." He insists that the aim of the Tea Party movement isn't to isolate the other parties and that, in fact, he shares some ideals with Democrats.[16]

"I think the interesting thing is that a lot of the things the Tea Party talk about are very popular with Democrats and Independents. We talk about term limits. You poll a balanced budget amendment you find that an enormous amount of Independents and Democrats support term limits and a balanced budget," Paul said.[17]

Rand Paul, however, has been censured by some for objecting to the Americans with Disabilities Act and some Civil Rights legislation because it tells owners of private businesses things they can and can't do. His objection to the recent health care legislation is that it orders Americans to purchase a product. He calls this a form of the government overreaching its mandate from the people. It is important to recognize that Paul is, unequivocally, not a racist and not someone who wishes to discriminate against handicapped people.

Paul also shares some values with the Libertarians. His father, Ron Paul, was Libertarian Party candidate for U.S. president in 1988 but has been a Republican Congressman from Texas since 1997. He did not vote for the 2002 Iraq War Resolution and believes the United

States should withdraw from the United Nations. Ron Paul's name has been associated with the Tea Party.

In the 2009 Conservative Political Action Conference Presidential Preference straw poll for the 2012 election, Paul tied 2008 GOP vice presidential candidate Sarah Palin for third place with 13 percent of the vote, behind fellow former candidate Mitt Romney (first) and Louisiana governor Bobby Jindal (second).[18]

- In the 2010 CPAC straw poll, Ron Paul came out on top, decisively winning with 31 percent, followed distantly by Mitt Romney, Sarah Palin, and Tim Pawlenty of Minnesota, among others.[19]
- In the 2010 Southern Republican Leadership Conference straw poll, Paul finished second place with 24 percent of the vote (438 votes), behind only Mitt Romney (with 439 votes).[20]

The Libertarian Party advocates downsizing the federal government, minimally regulated *laissez-faire* markets, strong civil liberties, minimally regulated migration across borders, and noninterventionism in foreign policy that respects freedom of trade and travel to all foreign countries.[21]

Another person to watch for on the political scene is Wayne Allyn Root, chairman of the Libertarian National Congressional Committee. He has a large following and is the author of *The Conscience of a Libertarian: Empowering the Citizen Revolution with God, Guns, Gambling & Tax Cuts,* published by John Wiley & Sons and released in 2009.

The Libertarian Party has for several years been the third largest political party in the United States. Some wealthy Libertarians have provided financing for Tea Party events.

TEA PARTY FUNDING

Have you heard of David H. Koch? He and his brother Charles have, behind the scenes, given tens of millions of dollars to right-wing causes, including propaganda campaigns against the federal government and President Obama. To be fair, they are also philanthropists who have given millions to cancer research and such organizations as the American Ballet Theatre, the Lincoln Center, the American Museum of Natural History and the Metropolitan Museum of Art.[22]

The Kochs own Koch Industries of Wichita, Kansas, with annual revenues of about a hundred billion dollars. They operate oil refineries in Alaska, Texas and elsewhere, control thousands of miles of pipeline and own companies which produce Brawny paper towels, Georgia-Pacific lumber, Dixie cups and other household items. Forbes ranks it as the second largest private company in the nation. The Koch fortune is thought to be bested by only those of Bill Gates and Warren Buffett.[23]

To have that much money, then want lower personal and corporate taxes at the expense of the ordinary U.S. citizen seems a bit over the top. They have some things they want government to do. Topping the list are drastically cutting back social services for the needy and much less oversight of industry, primarily when it is regulation designed to keep the environment clean.

Koch Industries was named one of the top ten air polluters in the nation by the University of Massachusetts Political Economy Research Institute. A Greenpeace report billed the company a "kingpin of climate science denial." The Kochs underwrite a huge network of think tanks, foundations, and political front groups in order to protect their own business interests. They also helped finance the fight against Obama's health care reform. The founder of a nonpartisan watchdog group who has been in Washington since Watergate said he had never seen anything like the Kochs "pattern of lawbreaking and political manipulation."[24]

Here's an example of Koch manipulation of the American people. The Koch-funded Americans for Prosperity Foundation sponsored a July 4, 2010 weekend summit called Texas Defending the American Dream. The event was advertised in advance as "a populist uprising against vested corporate power" and said, "Today, the voices of average Americans are being drowned out by lobbyists and special interests." The 500 people who attended were warned about the Obama Administration's "socialist vision for the country" during what was really a training session for Tea Party activists. There was, of course, no warning that "in part, this is a grassroots citizens' movement brought to you by a bunch of oil billionaires," said David Axelrod, senior adviser to President Obama.[25]

The Kochs deny any connection to the Tea Party, but the training session was organized by Peggy Venable, who draws a salary from Americans for Prosperity and who has been affiliated with Koch-funded groups since 1994. Venable told the trainees "We love what the Tea Parties are doing, because that's how we're going to take back America," and the misguided crowd cheered. They went home with lists of elected officials to target.[26]

There were other speakers. Some of the anti-Obama rhetoric was so outrageous, hateful, and over the top that no responsible American patriot would repeat it.

According to Jane Mayer in her August 30, 2010 *New Yorker* article about the Kochs, although they deny a connection to the Tea Party and say no Tea Party has ever approached them, Venable said David Koch was the chairman of her organization's board, and that she had met the Kochs.

One of the most telling statements was made by a Republican campaign consultant who had done research on behalf of Charles and David Koch. Here's what he had to say about the Tea Party:

> The Koch brothers gave the money that founded it. It's like they put the seeds in the ground. Then the rainstorm comes, and the frogs come out of the mud—and they're our candidates![27]

Obviously the Kochs are manipulating Tea Party members who may have no idea that these billionaire industrialist brothers are funding the Tea Party movement because of their own economic interests. The Tea Party may be a grass-roots organization, but it certainly is not a group of populists working to improve the government. Populists are interested in having the government work in the best interests of American citizens. The capitalist Koch brothers want it to serve the needs of big business. There is a world of difference between those stances.

Where does Sarah Palin weigh in on this issue? What does she think real populists want? Does she think the interests of big business are the same as the interests of her followers? She speaks in such general terms that it is difficult to discern if she sees through the Koch agenda or whether she even knows or cares about it.

CONCLUSIONS AND QUESTIONS

Most of the conclusions people make around the military industrial complex are only theoretical, but they give rise to many questions:

- Are foreigners helping shape American policy by serving on the boards of huge international corporations, policy-shaping organizations such as the Rand Corporation, and global money handlers such as the Carlyle Corporation?
- Is the apparent Republican versus Democrat adversarial role in running the United States really a sham?
- Does anyone really think that Sarah Palin, insulated in Alaska most of her life, really understands the workings of the military industrial complex? Does this mean that if she runs for president, she is being backed by the New World Order neo-conservatives? Would this make her a puppet? If so, how many puppets are already running countries around the world?
- Are the newly arrived Tea Party members so focused on disemboweling the federal government and transferring power, politics, and public agencies to the state level that they are ignoring the military industrial complex and the behind-the-scenes forces of globalization?
- If President Obama's hands are tied, was he clued in before he launched his presidential campaign, or was this a shock-and-no-awe discovery?

THE NEW POPULISTS

There is a burgeoning populist movement that wants to take back America but, unlike the Tea Party, it doesn't want to dismantle government but to clean it up, stabilize it, and make it truly responsive to its citizens by taking power away from such influences as the banking and insurance industries and multinational corporations.

The Democratic Party has traditionally been the party of the people. The Republican Party seems to have wrested that role away from the Democrats. Now the Tea Party, plus Sarah Palin and her followers, are taking the populist rhetoric to new extremes, some of them downright scary if you include remarks made and placards waved by the more militant members of the self-styled patriot movement. Populism is a political and social agenda that historically, has pitted the ordinary people against the so-called elite who control the government.

"There's one big difference between real populism and what the Tea Party thing is—real populists understand that government has become a subsidiary of corporations," says journalist and radio personality Jim Hightower of Texas. "So, you can't say let's get rid of government. You need to be saying let's take over government," he continues.[28]

Hightower, a populist historian and advocate, broadcasts daily radio commentary heard across America and publishes a monthly newsletter called the *Hightower Lowdown*. His latest books are *Thieves in High Places: They've Stolen Our Country and It's Time to Take it Back*, published in 2003, and *Swim Against the Current: Even a Dead Fish Can Go With the Flow*, which came out in 2008.[29]

To Hightower, populism is not just an outburst of rhetoric by angry citizens. "Certainly it is not anger funded and organized by corporate front groups, as the initial Tea Party effort is," he explains. Instead, he describes his brand of populism as getting people out of the grip of the corporate power that is crippling our economy, fouling our environment and overpowering our government.[30]

THE GILDED AGE

The Industrial Revolution brought power, wealth, and stature to the United States. This was an era of rapid economic and population growth that fueled our nation's emergence as a superpower. It was the age of wealthy railroad barons, manufacturing moguls, and banking kingpins. Then, as now, the wealthy elite exercised their power in the halls of government, flexing their financial muscle power.

It was also a time period during which the gap between the "haves" and the "have nots" widened considerably…that is, until the people rebelled in a populist movement that spawned co-ops, labor unions, and government regulations to protect the people from the excesses of those who lived in palatial mansions along the Hudson and in places like Newport, Rhode Island. Those were the Astors, the Vanderbilts, the Rockefellers, as well as Andrew Mellon, Andrew Carnegie, and many others.

The United States entered the twentieth century leading the world in industrial productivity and per capita income. New factories in industrial towns and cities—primarily in the northeast—hired and trained unskilled workers from rural areas, as well as immigrants from many European countries. Coal mining and steel production workers had backbreaking jobs and deplorable work conditions but minted more millionaires. United States Steel, formed by financier J.P. Morgan, became the nation's first billion-dollar corporation.[31]

"RAISE LESS CORN AND MORE HELL"

A series of droughts in the 1880s united farmers who were told by populist writer and activist Mary Elizabeth Least to "raise less corn and more hell." Working with sympathetic southern Democrats and small parties in the west, the Farmer's Alliance sought political power and coalesced as the Populist Party. The 1890 elections brought the new party into power-sharing coalitions in several states and sent several Populist senators and representatives to Congress.

The first Populist Convention in 1892 brought together delegates from not only farmers' organizations, but also from labor and reform groups whose goal was to reform what they regarded as a U.S. government manipulated by the financial interests of industrial and commercial entities. There was hostility to banks and railroads. The political group emanating from this grassroots movement was known as both "The People's Party" and "the Populists." Both "titles" were used in more modern times for movements, such as communism, which in no way shared the same motivation and ideals of America's late nineteenth century populist movement.[32]

Historians do not agree on the substance, motivation, goals, and accomplishments of the early American populist movement. Liberal scholars admire the Populists for their attacks on banks and railroads, as well as their determination to take on a government dominated by business interests. Others see a close link between the Populists and the Progressives of 1900–1912.

It is true that Teddy Roosevelt, the product of a wealthy family and a Republican, sympathized with the Populists and espoused some of their ideas. During his presidency (1901–1909), he tried to move the Republican Party toward a Progressive philosophy but failed to do so. Some leading Progressives, however, made clear that they were not of the Populist persuasion.[33]

Whether any Populist ideas made their way into the Democratic Party is debatable. Some historians see the Populists as forward-looking liberal reformers. Others characterize them as reactionaries who wanted to restructure American politics.

TODAY'S POPULIST MOVEMENT

The near economic meltdown of the U.S. economy, which started during the Bush presidency and got the alarmed Obama Administration off to a rocky start, has spawned a new look at the size, power, and impact of multinational corporations.

The fact that the Obama Administration felt the necessity to bail out the banks and automotive industries, using the rationale that because they were so big that if they failed the U.S. economy would fail, requires a new assessment.

"If you're too big to fail, you're too big period," says Hightower, adding that "And now they've become not only too big to fail, but too big to care."[34]

This remark holds within it a red flag for American citizens. Just as these corporations outsourced jobs to foreign countries where cheaper labor costs meant increased profits, so, too, can many of these mammoth business enterprises relocate their headquarters. As mentioned earlier, Halliburton, the world's second largest oilfield services company, has shifted its corporate headquarters to Dubai, where its chief executive officer is located, but will still keep some key people in its Houston offices.[35] Halliburton is well-linked with the right wing conservative New World Order movers and shakers. Its move is one more sign of increasing globalization in the business world.

In early 2010, the Dubai government also invited the United Nations to move its headquarters from New York to what is becoming the world's most modern and upscale city. Several corporate giants already have their regional hub office in Dubai because of their expanding customer base in the Middle East and Africa; it also places them closer to emerging Asian markets.

Hightower speaks for many Americans when he says he sees the central political issue to be the rise of corporate power. Overwhelming, overweening corporate power," he says, "that is running roughshod over the workaday people of the country. They think they're the top dogs and we're a bunch of fire hydrants," Hightower said. He makes clear that, over the long haul, the target is not, as the Tea Partiers and Libertarians claim, the government. "Instead, it is those who are pulling the strings of government," Hightower reports.[36]

ROLE OF THE DEMOCRATIC PARTY

Many are asking why the Democrats are not, in the interests of ordinary Americans, going after the corporate fat cats and their idea of what Hightower calls "tinkle-down economics" that do nothing to help the average American keep his or her house from foreclosure, or find a new job that will support a family.

Journalist Bill Moyers, during a PBS television interview of Jim Hightower, alluded to a mutual acquaintance that said the Republicans work for Wall Street and the Democrats are afraid to act against them. Traditionally, the Democrats represented unionized workers and Republicans represented businessmen. More recently, corporations have made end runs around the unions by outsourcing jobs and utilizing other employee practices not in the best interests of the workers.

Hightower finds it somewhat ironic that President Obama ran for office as an outsider and is trying to govern as an insider. "You can't do progressive government from the inside," Hightower concludes. His advice to the Democrats would be to have them do their own grass roots organizing to an even greater extent than they did during the Obama campaign for the presidency, then bring them inside the government so that stricter regulation of corporations could be achieved.[37] Such a movement would, of course, be anathema to conservative Republicans.

Hightower believes that through the decades it has been the activists like Thomas Paine, the suffragists, the abolitionists, the populists, members of the labor movement, and Martin Luther King who have extended democracy.

The Hightower rhetoric is just as folksy as that of Sarah Palin, but unlike her, he doesn't toss patriotic slogans around or speak in generalities. Here are two examples:[38]

> You know, that agitator after all is the center post in the washing machine that gets the dirt out. So, we need a lot more agitation. Bill Moyers: "So, is that what you mean when you say the water won't clear up until we get the hogs out of the creek?"
> Hightower: "That's right. They are in the creek. And, they're fouling our environment, our political and economic waters. And you don't get a hog out of the creek, Bill, by saying 'Here, hog, here hog'…you got to put your shoulder to it and shove it out of the creek."

Where is the Populist movement now? It is at the zip code level. Fed-up citizens across America are going beyond anger and ranting. They are often organizing others and taking on some aspect of corporate power. Many of their victories aren't seen as political; instead, they are civic action. More and more privately owned restaurants are featuring locally grown produce. Some consumer groups are primarily buying locally produced goods and products manufactured in America. In some small communities, where locally owned banks have been swallowed up by larger regional or national banks, people are shifting to local credit unions.

In October of 2009, 5,000 people rallied in Chicago outside the convention of the American Bankers Association. They would like to see the big banks "busted up." In April of 2010, thousands marched on Wall Street. They wanted the government on their side, fighting their battles because the economic system was working against them. Similar protests took place in San Francisco, North Carolina, and Kansas City.

Larry Ginter, a member of Iowa Citizens for Community Improvement, said, "If you've seen your pensions or retirement take a hit, stand up. Dissent is apple pie and ice cream. If you think it's time to put people first and hold banks accountable, stand up. His group fights for fair wages, housing, healthcare, the elderly, family farmers and the environment."[39]

COMMON DREAMS

CommonDreams.org, operating out of a Web site of the same name, calls itself "a national nonprofit, progressive, non partisan citizens' organization founded in 1997." Describing itself as "a powerful online voice for change in America," it claims to have "millions of monthly readers" and "one of the top progressive Web sites."[40]

This organization creates political organizing tools, plus models for internet activism. It publishes news stories of interest to progressives, plus ideas and opinions of progressive writers and activists. "CommonDreams.org is a must in my life and work," says Bill Moyers, the creator of the PBS TV show *Bill Moyers' Journal*.[41]

This excerpt from the organization's Web site describes its dream[42]:

- We are hundreds of thousands strong.
- We are united by our common dreams of peace and security, equal opportunity, and meaningful participation in our society.
- We are energized by our passionate belief that these dreams should be within reach of everyone. Regardless of race, gender, or status.

There are like-minded organizations across America that have an online presence. Members do not want to tear down the American government. Instead, they want to make it more responsive to American citizens. They are concerned about the nation's debt and continued deficit spending but are willing to work from inside the system rather than by attacking it from the outside. They are more disappointed than angry and do not use incendiary language.

THE SUMMING UP

In considering a rebirth of populism, there are messages to ponder. Some are a bit hazy and some are crystal clear. Here are some of those thoughts.

- It is important to distinguish between movements that *are* populist and those that simply *borrow* populist ideas.
- If the centerpiece of populism is that democracy should reflect the pure, undiluted will of the people, this ideology can cross party lines and come to rest at several points along the left-centrist-right political spectrum.
- It is dangerous to consider populism as pitting ordinary people against their government. This can lead to revolution. History chalks up several bloody revolutions of this type.
- Do today's U.S. citizens have so many different views of what they feel the government should do for its citizens that it is nearly impossible to come up with a list of what the average person would consider the functions of an ideal government?
- Is today's government alien to its citizens? Is it an institution that needs to be harnessed and reined in, or is it still the citizens' government because they paid for it, built it, and now need to get together to improve it?

The recent Tea Party movement could certainly be understood as an antigovernment movement. Many observers feel, however, that it has been co-opted by millions of dollars of financing from right-wing conservatives whose agenda favors globalization and supporting the giant multinational corporations by doing away with government regulations that cost them money but protect the American people. These ultaconservative Republicans appear to be using the Tea Party as a front group.

Looked at in this perspective, it seems as though many of Sarah Palin's followers, who want good jobs, opportunities for their children, and a comfortable retirement income, should be among the Populists who want the government on their side, working for them, instead of being at the beck and call of those business interests who are responsible for outsourcing millions of jobs and, at any moment, can pick up their toys and move their headquarters to another country, leaving the U.S. economy in a shambles.

It would be helpful if Sarah could shed some light on this, making clear how she thinks a government heavily controlled by the rich and powerful can help Main Street America and those already victimized by loss of work, lost homes and dwindling opportunities.

> *"All men are created equal." "Government by consent of the governed." "Give me liberty or give me death." And those are not just clever words, and those are not just empty theories. In their name Americans have fought and died for two centuries and tonight around the world they stand there as guardians of our liberty risking their lives. Those words are promised to every citizen that he shall share in the dignity of man. This dignity cannot be found in a man's possessions. It cannot be found in his power or in his position. It really rests on his right to be treated as a man equal in opportunity to all others. It says that he shall share in freedom. He shall choose his leaders, educate his children, (and) provide for his family according to his ability and his merits as a human being.*[43]
>
> *~ President Lyndon B. Johnson, March 15, 1965*

CHAPTER FIVE

SARAH PALIN'S PATRIOTISM: WHICH WAY TO SLICE IT?

"Joey: You can't have Thanksgiving without turkey. That's like Fourth of July without apple pie." ~ American TV show Friends

Sarah Palin exudes patriotism, even in the same breath in which she declares America is ready for a revolution. That's how we got our democracy, isn't it? By means of that first Boston Tea Party, the shots at Lexington and Concord heard round the world, and those first American patriots that fought in and won the American Revolution, so we could have freedom. Right story but the wrong comparison.

When Sarah says we're ripe for revolution, it's time to take another look.

That first American Revolution was by American colonies against England, their mother country. The ancestors of many of these patriots had left England for America more than a century earlier to begin a new life. The Revolutionary War, which helped birth our democracy, made the United States a new nation.

So what is the revolution Palin refers to against? If Sarah Palin's sympathies lie with those of her followers who want our present federal government decapitated and dismantled, this revolution would be against our existing government. As long as we have a democracy, that government belongs to our nation's citizens. That revolution, then, would have to be against some of us. That's an internal revolution of some Americans against other Americans.

Nearly every time a democracy has had such an internal revolution, it has been replaced by a dictatorship. The American Civil War is a major exception. Our American Revolution against England was fought to usher in a democracy not to cause polarization among our people.

The ultimate injustice that could be done to us, America's patriots, is to have a President Palin redefine patriotism to mean patriots are people who would support her administration policy, procedures and activities. Many citizens would refuse to have their patriotism redefined for something that sounds closer to nationalism than patriotism.

THE BUSH ADMINISTRATION: REDEFINING PATRIOTISM

The Bush Administration already tried to define patriotism for the nation. It was a very simplistic definition. You were patriotic if you supported the president and a war that was supposed to bring democracy and freedom to Iraq and Afghanistan. You were unpatriotic if you did not.

Some George Bush kin had something to say about this and allied matters during the run up to the 2004 presidential election campaign. They described themselves as *Bush Relatives for Kerry* and *the other patriots*.

THE OTHER PATRIOTS

Samuel Prescott Bush House was a spokesperson for the group. He was named for his great-grandfather, Samuel Prescott Bush (1863–1948), an American industrialist. This Samuel P. Bush is also a great-grandfather of former President George W. Bush. The present Samuel descends from the elder Samuel's daughter, Mary (Bush) House; President George W. Bush descends from the elder Samuel's son, Prescott Sheldon Bush.[1]

When this stand was taken by Bush relatives, George W. was running for his second presidential term. Here's what the president's second cousin, Samuel P.B. House, had to say about patriotism:[2]

> Our president and his supporters have tried to shape the label of a "patriot" as someone who does not question the policies or practices of his administration when the country is at war.

As someone who considers himself a patriot, I do not know how to understand the "patriotism" of our president. I find it difficult to understand the patriotism behind giving tax breaks to corporations that export jobs overseas, leaving well-meaning and hard-working folks at home without a solid chance to support themselves.

I find it incomprehensible that patriotism of the brand our president practices includes ravaging our environmental policies, resulting in an immediate and lasting degradation of the environment for the foreseeable future, hurting my children and their children, the future patriots of this country. How is it patriotic to give a series of tax breaks to the very wealthiest of individuals at a time of war when, at the time our president assumed office, we were well on the way to being solvent as a country? How is it "patriotic" to create the No Child Left Behind Act and then withhold the money set aside for its implementation, educationally neglecting our own children?

Members of this Bush relatives group who called themselves the other patriots, plus others who held similar ideas, had this to say: [3]

- We are patriots who fear Bush administration policy has harmed the environment, made inroads on our civil rights and robbed our pockets.
- We are the patriots who were alarmed when our country went to war without the consent of the United Nations and NATO allies.
- We are the patriots who were ashamed when this administration did not keep its promises to the people of Afghanistan and Iraq, and embarrassed us by the inhumane treatment of the Abu Ghraib prisoners.
- We are patriots who take our citizenship seriously and devote time to being well informed on issues that concern the government of our nation.
- We are not members of the extreme left or the extreme right. We do not visit "Bush-hater" sites on the Internet, but we do read a variety of mainstream newspapers, magazines, and reports.

- We do not, as patriots, like having our patriotism defined by a government that is out of touch with large groups of its citizens...a government led by a president without a clear mandate who squeaked through the 2000 election.
- We object to having our morality classified by a government that we feel has a fuzzy view of why the framers of our Constitution insisted on separation of church and state. Very few of us belong to the fundamentalist Christian churches, but many of us are either Roman Catholics or members of the more traditional Christian churches. Some of us adhere to non-Christian religions.
- Our faith-based initiatives and compassionate deeds take place on the community level in a country which has more than 35 million people classified as poor, according to the Census Bureau report released in 2004. *(Editor's Note: A more recent census estimate puts it as forty-four million in poverty. That is one out of every seven Americans.)*
- We are ashamed of an administration that praises American soldiers while they cut veteran benefits.
- We are angry with Washington officials who pretend their assault on the environment is for our own good when it is apparent that many environmental policies benefit the marketers of oil, natural gas and electricity, as well as their big business clients.
- We are patriots who resent being patronized by a president and other government leaders who appear to assume we are not well-informed, concerned citizens when they issue deceptive information on the causes and costs of war, or tell us our economy is improving while the jobless rate increases.

"Let's hope there are enough of us to make a difference."[4]

PATRIOTISM IS MORE THAN SLOGANS AND FLAG-WAVING

The declaration of patriotism by those Bush relatives still resonates with many Americans. Why? Because patriotism is more than supporting soldiers and pledging allegiance to the flag. Patriotism is an individual thing. It is composed of our ideals. It relates to what we think our role is when it comes to stewardship of our planet and compassion for other people. It has ingredients that come from how we define freedom, equality, and justice.

American citizens long were seen as freedom-loving, intelligent, compassionate, and productive people who carved out a land of opportunity. That American dream, however, has started to fray around the edges and become less attainable for both present day immigrants and American-born citizens. Why?

- A supportive family framework isn't present. Many immigrants come to the United States alone to find work and send money back home.
- The accelerated divorce rate has resulted in single-parent families wherein the wage earner has little time for parenting.
- The dignity and respect felt by most working Americans has given way to a weakened work ethic because of a paralyzing four-generation welfare program that makes it difficult to exit the poverty cycle.
- Unlike earlier immigrants, people refuse to work their way up to a good job; they regard entry-level jobs as demeaning.
- Jobs are not plentiful. In this changing job market unskilled work has either been outsourced to countries where people are eager to have these jobs or is done by migrant workers and illegal immigrants.
- The high United States poverty rate has produced a class of alienated citizens who are angry because they feel they are entitled to more.

There are millions of American patriots scattered from Maine to New Mexico and Seattle to Miami. Bands of us crisscross America. We have a president, a vice president, legislators, a secretary of defense, a secretary of state, and an attorney general. Some of them were elected by us, and all of them have a mandate to work on behalf of patriotic Americans. Yet, the profile we have of many of our leaders is tainted by constant evidence that their highest priority is partisan politics. Instead of sitting down to solve complex problems affecting our nation, they squabble and criticize each other. They are already preparing for the next election campaign. They aren't working for us, the citizen patriots.

PATRONIZING THE PATRIOTS

In the most recent Bush Administration some of our elected and appointed officials did more than deceive us. In a patronizing, arrogant manner they misread, misrepresented, and misled America's patriots. They fought a war in the wrong country for the wrong reasons. They stole our own country blind, driving us into the biggest debt we ever had—so big that the problems it caused, such as bank failures and widespread job losses, are difficult to fix. Lady Liberty should have been angrily clawing at the sky from her pedestal in New York Harbor.

We no longer heartily welcome the oppressed. Under the Bush Administration, Haitians seeking asylum were, contrary to the rules of international law, confined in detention centers. That included children! This was against rights enforceable by the Inter-American Court of Human Rights.

We defied the United Nations, astounding traditional European allies with our audacity. They were shocked when Americans reelected a president who lied to them about reasons for the Iraq "shock and awe" attack and its aftermath...stunned that more than half the voting electorate would affirm a president who plunged the country into monumental debt.

The United States spat at the Geneva conventions, violated international law, and tried to degrade basic human dignity by mistreating prisoners in Guantanamo and at Abu Ghraib.

Give Lady Liberty the world's poor, the world's hungry? We better start with our own. They are now more than 10 percent of our population.

DEFINING PATRIOTISM

Who would the patriots be in Sarah Palin's revolution? Aren't all Americans patriots? Maybe and maybe not. Perhaps we don't have the same definition of patriotism.

What is patriotism? Is there a patriotism that is not nationalistic? Here are thumbnail answers summarizing the thoughts of various thinkers who have brought some expertise to the subject. None of them are necessarily right or wrong. Instead, their remarks depict the diversity and complexity of how individuals view the ingredients or ideals that they individually package as their patriotism.[5]

Dr. John Schaar, professor emeritus of political philosophy, University of California at Santa Cruz:

There are two large camps of patriots. The first group, rooted in radical ideologies of the French Revolution, worship national power and national greatness, nearly always expressed as power over other peoples. This voice has been as clamorous and continuous in our own country as in many others.

The line from Col. Alexander Hamilton to Lt. Col. Oliver North is strong and pure. The other company of patriots does not march to military time. It prefers the gentle strains of "America the Beautiful" to the strident cadences of "Hail to the Chief." This patriotism is rooted in the love of one's own land and people, as well as love of the best ideals of one's own culture and tradition.

These patriots find no glory in puffing up their country by pulling others down. This patriotism has quiet pleasures and steady, unpretentious service. This patriotism, too, has deep roots and long continuity in our history. Thomas Jefferson, Abraham Lincoln, and Martin Luther King Jr. were among its spokesmen.

We should not be surprised to now hear voices lamenting the country's failures to live up to its own best ideals...the fullest possible freedom and the most equal justice for all. The voice of this patriotism is often temporarily shouted down by the battle cries of the first company, but it has never been stilled.

Floyd Abrams, constitutional lawyer:

The left has always had a problem with patriotism. No one has blessed America more movingly than Woody Guthrie, but generally the left seems sour on America and more sour still about patriotism. It's not that the right hasn't routinely substituted flag-waving for reason...or, even that a dumb, smug sort of

Americanism has been used to justify every national sin of which we've been capable.

Adlai Stevenson understood that patriotism could rightly be defined as the celebration of "the right to hold ideas that are different–the freedom of man to think as he pleases." Why, then, the resistance on the left to patriotic appeals? Why such a crabbed view of Americanism at its best Why not celebrate Justices Marshall and Blackmun? Or the 200th anniversary of the Bill of Rights? Or a message of freedom beamed from America to the rest of the world—often received there but too often denigrated here?

Richard A. Cloward, professor, Columbia University School of Social Work, and Frances Fox Piven, professor, City University of New York:

We take patriotism to mean love of nation and the loyalty that follows. My country, right or wrong. It is hard to see how thinking people justify blind loyalty. Considered historically, patriotism is plainly dangerous, helping to unleash military rampages in the name of nation.

When leaders appeal to patriotism, they mobilize citizens by invoking foreign threats that cannot be assessed by ordinary people, except sometimes when it is too late, as in the aftermath of war. In the process, not only are people made to sacrifice lives and resources to the contests of these state-makers, but the emotions generated overwhelm popular capacities for a reasoned and conflictual domestic politics.

William Sloane Coffin, former Yale chaplain, pastor of Riverside Church, New York, civil rights activist, and, he says, committed by his faith to global peace and social justice.

The worst patriots are those who hold certainty dearer than truth; who, in order to spare themselves the pain of thought, are willing to inflict untold sufferings on others.

If uncritical lovers of their country are the most dangerous of patriots, loveless critics are hardly the best. Surely the best patriots are those who carry on not a grudge fight, but a lover's quarrel with their country. The main burden of their quarrel in today's and tomorrow's world must be to persuade fellow citizens that *the planet itself is now at risk. Everyone's security depends on everyone else's. No one is safe until all are safe. Beyond saluting the flag, led us pledge allegiance to the earth, and to the flora, fauna and human life that it supports; one planet, indivisible, with clean air, soil and water, liberty, justice and peace for all.*

Martin Duberman, biographer, playwright, and professor of history, City University of New York.

Who isn't a patriot? Everybody claims the designation and loyalty to the particular set of ideals and institutional arrangement they choose to identify as the essence of Americanism. Those of us who deplore the country's descent into macho militarism refuse to cede patriotism to those who equate it with George Bush's policies...we hold to an insistence that the needs of people come before the display of hardware, however technologically brilliant. We hold that all human life is valuable.

The view that some nationalities, races, religions, sexual orientations, and genders are more valuable than others disgraces the notion of democracy–just as the growing disparities in wealth and privilege in our own country discredit the notion that we are the exemplars of democracy. We hold to an insistence that the rights of conscience take precedence over the profits of business. We hold to a celebration internationally of human diversity, and we champion the integrity of indigenous cultures over imperialistic demands for conformity. Obviously, we're the real patriots. How come THEY can't understand that?

Richard Falk, Professor of international relations, Princeton University:

Confusing patriotism with unconditional support for government policy does core damage to the meaning of citizenship, especially during time of war. Wartime accentuates the pressure to be a patriot, especially if one's country is in physical danger. At times of national emergency, arguably, unity may be relevant to survival. U.S. wars since World War II have not been of this character. These wars have been distant encounters in the third world, of dubious legality and morality...to mingle patriotic fervor with militarism is pernicious and dangerous for us all.

As citizens in the nuclear age, we must struggle harder to convince others that the true patriot is now, above all, dedicated to peace and justice, to diplomatic solutions and to a foreign policy respectful of international law and of the United Nations so long as it acts within its constitutional mandate.

Given the power and wealth of the United States, our pressing need is for a nationalist humility and the forming of a more global political identity that is engaged in the great work of solidarity with peoples everywhere, first of all here at home, who are working to overcome the afflictions of humanity.

Howard Fast, novelist and columnist for the New York Observer:

Patriotism in its most common usage is best defined as the last refuge of scoundrels, who label every infamy and abomination as patriotism. Let me list some of the things these scoundrels define as patriotism: fighting wars of aggression thousands of miles away, fighting wars of colonial oppression, poisoning the atmosphere with auto emissions and pollution and acid rain, ruthlessly destroying the forests, promoting racism as a way of winning elections, cutting away at civil rights, lying about every question of the public good, bleeding the people dry and destroying all that America stands for with an armaments industry large beyond reason or need, spending our wealth on armaments while our cities crumble, our infrastructure disintegrates and our schools are left without teachers. Patriotism as a word applies to true love of one's country and a code of conduct that echoes such love.

Rev. Jesse L. Jackson, president, National Rainbow Coalition

Too often those who dare expand our nation's democracy and make it true to our principles are victims of naked aggression, aggression led not by street fighters, but by the White House, Congress and the courts...those who have fought for the highest and best principles of our country, the true patriots, have been vilified. The true patriots invariably disturb the comfortable and comfort the disturbed...We must never relinquish our sense of justice for a false sense of national pride. "My country, right or wrong," is neither moral nor intelligent. Those who fight for civil

rights, open housing, environmental laws, peace and interna-
tional cooperation, and veterans of domestic wars—the true
patriots—receive no parades.

When the *Nation*, one of America's oldest news magazines, cel-
ebrated its 125th anniversary in 1991, it published a special July 15
issue on patriotism. The above thoughts on patriotism first appeared
in that edition; they have been condensed for use in this book. A
decade later, following the 9/11 tragedy, the magazine took another
look at those inspiring thoughts and posted them on its Web site,
where they can still be accessed.

"Guard against the 'impostures' of pretended patriotism," said
George Washington who, a faltering Sarah Palin told TV interviewer
Glenn Beck, was her favorite founding father. When he first asked
who her favorite founding father was, Palin gave the same answer
she gave interviewer Katie Couric when asked what newspapers
she read: "All of them." Beck pushed until he got a name out of
her.

We have poked our noses into a lot of pigeonholes and found that
patriotism is not a simple slogan, but instead a complex fabric woven
of various ideals. Instead of flag waving, it is more an attempt to stitch
together a national fabric, an American tapestry that depicts us as
moral, humane, and responsible citizens.

During two World Wars we were a people who understood that
our freedom, our underlying Constitution based upon human rights,
and our democracy, where diversity, equality, and justice take priority, were not one-way streets lined with signs for or against gun laws,
abortion and other single-issue demands of segments of our society. Then, we were united, not divided. How can we get that positive
image back? Shouldn't our elected leaders start work on that instead
of dissing each other?

We can easily find various definitions of patriotism—some we
agree with and some we don't. The conclusion? One of the freedoms we enjoy is to be patriotic in our own way; one of our obliga-
tions under that freedom is to allow and respect the right of others
to define their patriotism in their own way. We should not let any
leader—President Obama, Sarah Palin, or anyone else—define our
patriotism for us. Once a leader defines patriotism for all the citizens,

we are traveling that road to demagoguery that the experience of other nations should warn us against.

AMERICA'S NEW SUPER HERO: SUPER PATRIOT

We are not the wonderful society we were fifty or sixty years ago. We are a polarized nation whose worldwide image has been tarnished. We are so at war against each other that in some segments of America a man who crashed his plane into an IRS office building is a hero. We live in a land where several hundred thousand citizens call themselves sovereign citizens and believe they are above the law. They interpret freedom as the right to do as they wish, regardless of its impact on others.

DEPARTMENT OF HOMELAND SECURITY REPORT ON RIGHT-WING EXTREMISM

A report prepared within the Department of Homeland Security and dated April 7, 2009 is titled "Rightwing Extremism: Current Economic and Political Climate Fueling Resurgence in Radicalization and Recruitment."[6]

The report is meant to brief law enforcement personnel and others charged with enforcement of security measures to protect the United States from domestic terrorism and allied threats. It was deemed important to give these professionals a greater understanding "of the phenomenon of violent radicalization in the United States" and is therefore a briefing document. It was not marked for distribution to the public, but copies have been obtained under the Freedom of Information Act and portions of the general public are aware of its content.

Its basic conclusion is that extremist group membership with radical ideologies has increased because of the global economic meltdown, the size of the United States debt, and the political climate that followed President Obama into the White House. It has no information on violent acts planned by domestic terrorists but emphasizes the stepped-up recruitment of members by extremist groups, concluding that current events may be facilitating the ability of domestic extremist groups to add new members.[7]

Threats from "white supremacist and violent antigovernment groups during 2009 were characterized as "largely rhetorical." The chief concern was that a prolonged economic downturn, accompanied by home foreclosures, loss of jobs, and unavailability of credit would cause fear and anger and radicalize victims of these negative circumstances. The election of the first African American president of the United States was also seen as a catalyst for racist hate groups to use to their advantage.[8]

Some more recent polls and the monitoring of extremist groups by the Southern Poverty Law Center have affirmed that these conditions exist and that current events have led to not only increased membership in extremist groups but also to the proliferation of such groups.

THE SOVEREIGN CITIZENS MOVEMENT

Police stopped a white minivan for a routine traffic check on May 20, 2010 in West Memphis, Arkansas. Within minutes both officers were killed and the driver of the minivan, Jerry Kane, and his son Joseph, sixteen, fled. West Memphis authorities say that as the officers questioned Jerry Kane, his son Joe suddenly leaped out of the minivan and opened fire on the officers with an AK-47 assault rifle. When his father drove off, teenager Joe was still firing his rifle from the van.[9]

More than an hour later, the Kanes' white van was spotted and surrounded in a Wal-Mart parking lot. When the Kanes tried to escape, a fish and wildlife officer rammed his truck into their vehicle. The Kanes began firing at the wildlife officer's cab at close range. Meanwhile, the police arrived, and Jerry and Joe Kane died in the ensuing gun battle.[10]

"Officers did what they could to save the lives of their fellow officers and themselves, and you know, it has not been a difficult call for this office to say that this was a justified shoot," said Mike Walden, the prosecuting attorney for the second judicial district in Arkansas.[11]

In his follow-up story, ABC Newsman Dan Harris said the father and son allegedly were "sovereign citizens" deeply immersed in "a secretive and dangerous subculture that believes American laws don't apply to them." Further investigation indicated that sovereign citizens are located nearly all over the United States and are believed to number in the hundreds of thousands.[12] This is not a new movement. Its members include Terry Nichols, one of three men convicted for the April 19, 1995 bombing of the federal office building in Oklahoma City, which claimed the lives of 168 people, and Andrew Joseph Stack III, who flew his small plane into the IRS offices in Austin, Texas.

J.J. McNab, a financial consultant who has been investigating sovereign citizens for several years and is writing a book on them, told ABC News that most members of this movement are white middle-aged men whose philosophy has been pieced together from random bits of the Constitution, the Bible, commercial law, and admiralty law. This mélange of information has convinced them that they don't have to pay taxes or legal debts. Some are self-styled modern day "freedom fighters" which, to them, means they are American superpatriots. This disturbing ABC News report ended on a frightening note—some sovereign citizens are already calling Jerry and Joe Kane "heroes."[13]

STEPPING STONES TO RADICALISM

The sovereign citizens and their ideas did not rise up out of nowhere. For decades, there have been highly educated people that believe our government has metamorphosed into something it was never meant to be. They view the present government structure in a negative fashion and are quick to compare it to what they believe was the better government we had before there were such things as social security, income taxes, Medicare, and welfare. They want to abolish our present government and replace it with a system whose chief function is to protect us as we exercise our freedoms individually in an unregulated society. They believe that our government's main value is to keep a standing army ready to protect us from foreign invaders.

A more detailed look at this can be found on the Web site of the Future of Freedom Foundation where there is a reasoned explanation of this view of government. Especially enlightening are Jacob Hornberger's explanation of the Constitution and the rule of law and the remarks in the section titled "What is Libertarianism?"

Hornberger's Foundation would not condone the criminal acts of sovereign citizens, but it is easy to see how some of the Libertarian philosophy could, in the hands of certain people, become more radicalized and lead to offshoots such as the sovereign citizens.

In addition, those who would like to replace our present government—and that includes some rather mainstream "states rights" adherents and more conservative members of the Republican Party—with a more constrained form of government do not appear to factor in to their arguments the more complex world in which we live. It is easy to see that complexities on almost every level of today's existence are a great contrast to the world that Thomas Jefferson lived in. Our highly advanced technology has bred layers of specialists and experts whose input is needed in order for the public at large to function.

This is a marked contrast to a century ago when government was much smaller. Surely, some of the growth in government is related to not only this added complexity but also to the need for a global focus at a time when people can cross the Atlantic or Pacific in just a few hours.

The reasons behind formation of the European Union and the impact that has had on individual countries should also be studied before taking the paring knife to our government. That the European nations felt a need for joint governmental functions in some ways contradicts any reasoning that the United States should be passing a multitude of governmental functions from the federal government to costly duplication on the level of the various states.

AN FBI BRIEFING ON SOVEREIGN CITIZENS

Sovereign citizens are antigovernment extremists who believe that even though they physically reside in this country, they are separate or sovereign from the United States. As a result, they believe they don't have to answer to any government authority, including courts, taxing entities, motor vehicle departments, or law enforcement, says an FBI report dated April 13, 2010.[14]

The FBI considers sovereign citizens a domestic terrorism threat. FBI officials across the nation now monitor sovereign citizens who don't pay taxes, hold their own illegal courts that issue warrants for judges and police officers, or clog up the official court system with frivolous lawsuits and liens against public officials to harass them.[15]

Sovereign citizens also use fake money orders, fake personal checks, and fake diplomatic identity cards claiming they are immune from prosecution. They indulge in these fraudulent practices, targeting government agencies, banks, and businesses.[16]

Not every action taken in the name of the sovereign citizen is a crime, says the FBI, but the list of illegal actions committed by members of these groups is extensive, the FBI reports, saying they have committed murder and physical assault, threatened judges, law enforcement professionals and government personnel, impersonated police officers and diplomats, used fake currency, passports, license plates and driver's licenses, and engineered various scams, including mortgage fraud.[17]

This FBI advisory notes that sovereign citizens are often confused with extremists from the militia movement. However, it says, while sovereign citizens sometimes use or buy illegal weapons, guns are secondary to their antigovernment, antitax beliefs. Guns and paramilitary training are paramount to militia groups.[18]

The FBI cites three recent cases involving sovereign citizens.[19] More details on each are available on the FBI Web site.

- In Sacramento, California, two sovereign citizens were convicted of running a fraudulent insurance scheme. Operating outside state insurance regulatory guidelines, the men set up their own company and sold lifetime memberships to customers, promising to pay any accident claims against their members. The company collected millions of dollars but paid out very few claims.
- In Kansas City, three sovereign citizens were convicted of taking part in a conspiracy using phony diplomatic credentials. They charged customers between $450 and $2,000 for a diplomatic identification card, which would bestow upon the holder "sovereign status," meaning they would enjoy diplomatic immunity from paying taxes and from being arrested by law enforcement officials.
- In Las Vegas, four men affiliated with the sovereign citizens movement were arrested by the Nevada Joint Terrorism Task Force on federal money laundering, tax evasion, and weapons charges. The investigation involved an under-

cover operation with two of the suspects laundering more than a million dollars from what they believed was a bank fraud scheme.

In other words, sovereign citizens think nothing of making ordinary U.S. citizens victims of their illegal moneymaking schemes.

The FBI Web site also includes Department of Justice news releases on the arrests and convictions of several sovereign citizens.

SOUTHERN POVERTY LAW CENTER REPORT

Hate groups are now rapidly growing in the United States, reports the Southern Poverty Law Center (SPLC). Their statistics and related material confirm conclusions reached by the nation's Department of Homeland Security.

The SPLC, located in Montgomery, Alabama, next year begins its fifth decade as an American legal advocacy organization. It is internationally known for its tolerance education programs, which reach thousands of school students, and for its legal victories against white supremacists.

The SPLC is also known for monitoring hate groups, militias, and extremist organizations. It classifies as hate groups those organizations that it has determined "have beliefs or practices that attack or malign an entire class of people, typically for their immutable characteristics." It says, "Extremists in the U.S. come in many different forms—white nationalists, antigay zealots, black separatists, racist skinheads, neo-Confederates, and more."[20]

An interesting aside: Since Obama's presidency began, various anti-Obama Web sites have accused him of being a Nazi or socialist. One of the hate groups in the SPLC database is the National Socialist Movement which has a neo-Nazi idealogy and is on the opposite end of the political spectrum from Obama. It has no tolerance for non-whites.[21]

The SPLC database is searchable by names of well-known extremists, by the ideologies of hate groups and by the names of extremist organizations.

Its latest report, issued in March of 2010, is titled "Rage on the Right" and is the cover story of the latest edition of the SPLC's award-winning quarterly magazine, the *Intelligence Report*.[22]

"The number of extremist groups in the United States exploded in 2009 as militias and other groups steeped in wild, antigovernment conspiracy theories exploited populist anger across the country and infiltrated the mainstream," the report warned. The report also said:[23]

- Antigovernment "patriot groups" that see the federal government as their enemy have become far more active.
- During 2009 the number of active "patriot" groups grew from 149 to 512 in number.
- Militias, the paramilitary arm of the "patriot" movement, grew the most. For every one that existed in 2008, there were three in 2009.
- Patriot group membership is increasing because people are angry over the nation's public debt, the troubled economy, and Obama initiatives his opponents have labeled as "socialist" or even "fascist," an ironic turn of events since some of the extremist groups are fascist in nature.
- The patriot movement has made significant inroads into conservative politics. (The SPLC clarifies that it does not regard the tea party groups as extremist hate groups, but believes some of their members have radical ideas, believe in groundless conspiracy theories, and have racist members.)
- The number of racist hate groups increased from a record high of 926 in 2008 to 932 in 2009, not a significant increase.
- There has been a surge in "nativist extremist" groups. These vigilante organizations that confront and harass suspected illegal immigrants grew from 173 groups in 2008 to 309 in 2009.
- Three strands of the radical right—hate groups, nativist extremist groups, and "patriot" organizations termed "the most volatile elements on the American political landscape"—increased their numbers from 1,248 groups in 2008 to 1,753 in 2009.

Responsible mainstream Americans believe this SPLC report and that of the Department of Homeland Security indicate an alarming trend that could have dire consequences for the American citizenry.

WHERE DOES SARAH PALIN FIT IN?

What does all of this have to do with patriotism or with Sarah Palin? The main cross current here is that these arguments about the size and function of government are inextricably tied to our definitions of freedom and our interpretation of both our Constitution and the rule of law. Those, in turn, to some extent affect how we look at patriotism and define it for ourselves. In addition, Sarah Palin's definition of patriotism has remained unclear. It is hard to identify its components once you get past the flag-waving and slogans.

Sarah Palin has attracted members of many fringe groups. If Sarah Palin in her quest for notoriety were to gather these militia groups around her for the revolution which she says is needed, our nation could be irreparably harmed.

If Sarah desires to have credibility with mainstream America and be a responsible leader, she needs to divorce herself from antigovernment extremists, especially those like the sovereign citizens, who do not believe in the rule of law. That she has not done so is alarming, especially as she has said America needs a revolution.

DEFINE YOUR PATRIOTISM FOR YOURSELF

Patriotism cannot be described as right or wrong, left or right. Patriotism is connected with our individual backgrounds, our upbringing, our experiences as citizens of this nation, what our lifestyle is, how our opinions have been molded, how we react to what our government is doing, and what our personal achievements, fears, prejudices, and goals are.

It is for all these reasons that we both need to define our own patriotism and compare or contrast it with signals our leaders give off about their patriotism.

There are things we need to know not only about Sarah Palin, but also about anyone who has a serious impact on the running of our government and in our personal lives. We need to size up the signals we get about how they have defined their own patriotism.

Flag waving and talking about patriotism is not enough. Indeed, flag waving can be a cover-up. Patriotism can be used by powerful people as a weapon to incite fear and anger. "My country right or wrong" is not patriotism. It is nationalism. The two are different.

We need to know whether Sarah Palin is privy to the top echelon's secrets and onboard with the hidden message, or instead a naïve and overly enthusiastic follower who, like millions of patriotic Americans, believes most things they are told. Part of Palin's message appears to be a sugar-coated one centered around a 1950s world of comfort, patriotism, and a simpler lifestyle. It was a world in which most moms stayed home to raise the kids, provide a good home life for their working husbands and, yes, bake apple pies, puddings, and layer cakes topped with delicious icing. It probably was a more wholesome world free from fears of a threatened planet, a crippling economy, and rampant crime.

Today, American patriots are found in all political parties, in both rural and urban environments, and in every occupation. These patriots come from every racial and religious background. They cannot be separated by color, creed, job title, or hometown.

Yet, some observers believe that Americans are now more divided than at any other time since the American War between the States, which great-grandparents from the southern states refused to call the Civil War.

Just as the racial divide is slipping into the past (or is it?), a dangerous political divide has grown up around us and among us. Unfortunately, it tries to politically combine politics and religion in a country whose seventeenth-century settlers left that combination in England to colonize what became the United States. Their descendants framed an American Constitution that called for the separation of church and state. Such men as Samuel Adams, John Hancock, Benjamin Franklin, and Thomas Jefferson insisted on that separation because they feared a one-religion political structure that would discriminate and ostracize some of its patriots based on their religious beliefs. European history is laced with examples of religious persecution by governments.

It is an unpatriotic act to accuse someone of not being patriotic because of differing religious beliefs.

Our nation's problems cannot be solved until all Americans make a unified effort to define a better world and become part of the solution. The United States was founded by patriots with a common vision. It can only continue with patriots at peace with each other who formulate a common vision flexible enough to contain the world we now live in.

Going Rogue is dedicated to "all patriots" and to "our women and men in uniform, past and present." Does that mean Catholic, Lutheran, and Episcopalian patriots? Does it mean gay and lesbian patriots? Does it mean patriots who practice birth control? More to the point in our present society: Does Sarah also include our Muslim citizens as patriots? Does that mean Jewish, Muslim, and Hindu men and women in uniform? Does it mean same sex couples in uniform? How about women in uniform who have abortions after being raped by fellow soldiers?

MUSLIMS IN THE U.S. ARMED FORCES

According to an article on the U.S. Department of Defense Web site, in 2001 there were between five and seven million Muslims in America and upward of 10,000 serving in the U.S. armed forces.[24]

Many of our Muslim soldiers have died on the battlefield. Tucked among the crosses at Arlington National Cemetery, are crescents, the symbol that marks Muslim graves. Among them is that of army captain Humayun Khan, who lured a suicide car bomb away from the men in his charge, saving their lives but giving up his own.[25] Army chaplain Capt. Abdul-Rasheed Muhammad is a Muslim Imam stationed at Walter Reed Army Medical Center in Washington. In his chaplaincy, he ministers to all faiths.[26] Muslims are so devout that many who work with them convert to Islam. That includes a Guantanamo guard and a West Point graduate. [27] Col. Douglas Burpee, the highest-ranking Muslim in the U.S. Marine Corps and a career officer, converted to Islam. Col. Burpee, who has flown planes in Afghanistan, was raised an Episcopalian and converted after he met an Egyptian woman named Hala when they were University of Southern California students. They married and now have five sons.[28]"

Those people who commit terrorism have just adopted the face of Islam. Nothing they say or do has anything to do with Islam, Burpee said, explaining, "The Taliban is a terrorist organization. They are bad people doing bad things, and they've attached religion to it. They are ruthless when it comes to killing people, but that's how you move helpless people around—you use fear."[29]

There are also Muslim women serving in our military. "Those terrorists must be reading a completely different Koran than the rest of us," said Marine Corps Capt. Aisha Bakkar-Poe. Bakkar-Poe is from Kentucky. Her father comes from Syria and her mother from the States.[30]

Army captain Arneshuia Balial, a Walter Reed Army Medical Center nursing instructor and a Muslim, said the terrorists claiming to act in the name of Islam was "like a knife through my heart. That people would practice Al-Islam but do deeds like what they've done. It's not true faith. Some people twist religion to the way they think," she said.[31]

SARAH PALIN'S PATRIOTISM

Sarah Palin, who often cites the Constitution and the American flag as the bedrock of her patriotism, often contradicts herself. In coming down hard against the construction of a Moslem community center near ground zero in New York, Sarah, along with many others, seems to have forgotten that the Constitution cites freedom of religion as one of the tenets on which our democracy was built. She seems to have overlooked and ignored millions of Muslim Americans and the sacrifices their children have made in service to their country and its flag. In addition to giving up their lives while serving with American forces in the Middle East, they also gave up their lives in Vietnam, the Korean Conflict and World War II.

No matter which way you slice it, Sarah Palin's true brand of patriotism needs a clearer definition. Is she aligned with the mainstream or is she building an alliance among so-called "patriot" antigovernment groups, including the law-violating hundreds of thousands strong sovereign citizens and dozens of neo-Nazi groups that certainly don't agree with her pro-Israel stance?

There are many contradictions in what one observer termed "the Sarah Palin Across America business." Writer David Carr said Palin "turned on a dime from politics" to a burgeoning media mogul who has made several million dollars from her book and media appearances, which include several lucrative TV specials yet to come.[32]

As Carr noted, Palin even ventures into unfriendly territory, including an appearance on the Oprah show which gave it Oprah's best ratings in two years.[33] So, instead of heading for the White House, is Sarah trying to become the next Oprah? Although Palin appears to be open and willing to spill her guts or say whatever crosses her mind, in reality she still is holding her most important cards close to her vest.

Keep watch as the Palin saga unfolds. In addition to putting together your own individual package as a patriot, try to see if you can discover those hopes, dreams, goals, ideals, cultural preferences, and lifestyle leanings that describe not what is going into Palin as a brand name but into Palin as a patriot.

CHAPTER SIX

SARAH, EVE, AND THE APPLE: IT ISN'T GRANDMOTHER'S PIE

"To a foreigner a Yankee is an American. To an American a Yankee is a Northerner. To a Northerner a Yankee is a New Englander. To a New Englander a Yankee is a Vermonter. To a Vermonter a Yankee is a person who eats apple pie for breakfast." ~ Journal of American Folklore

Many Americans over sixty are full of nostalgia. They would love to see America drift backward in time to those halcyon days of the 1950s. Life was simpler. Jobs were plentiful. A family could live on one income. The average person's stress level was minimal. You could buy a nice house for under $25,000 and a car for under $3,000. You knew your neighbors well enough to know whether you could trust them or not.

Those times are gone. Forever. Millions of Sarah Palins couldn't bring them back. Life in small town Alaska in many ways is not the average American lifestyle, even though computers, high healthcare costs and a bevy of twenty-first century stressors have intruded there. Today's complex problems are not simply solved. Some have accumulated and worsened over decades. They weren't created by any one president and can't be solved by a single president.

Conservative right-wingers who speak as though they are America's only patriots can only cause further division. Americans all over the nation who are not conservatives have family values, religious faith, and are top-grade patriots. The energy that goes into finger-pointing around such issues as abortion and gay marriage needs to be channeled into a unified vision of a cleaner, safer, and economically prosperous America whose citizens enjoy a more wholesome and less stressful way of life.

The United States is running out of time to come up with that vision and the strategy for implementing it. That vision cannot be of a 1950s vintage. It has to deal with this century's problems and the aspirations of all of America's patriots. Yes, all of America's patriots need to be channeling positive effort into meeting the challenges ahead of us.

This cannot be done while Sarah Palin pushes her "don't retreat, just reload" strategy. Instead, we need a unified effort. Cooperation. It cannot be reached while Palin and her supporters claim that President Obama's financial bailouts, the health care bill, and other initiatives are bankrupting America.

The reality is that the gross national debt hit a forty-seven-year low just as President Reagan was taking office. It climbed steadily under Reagan and G.H.W. Bush, declined under Clinton, and made a quick U-turn under G.W. Bush. The *Congressional Record* in April of 2000 cites an interesting U.S. Senate discussion of what was then a $5 trillion debt that required $1 billion a day of tax money to pay the interest.[1]

Sandbagging our president by presenting false information detracts from his ability to govern. Using untrue claims to fan the flames of anger, frustration, and fear is unpatriotic. It is not the American way. It also is not in the best interest of our country.

Many people say they fear socialism. Ironically, it is those people who most warn about it that are likely to set the stage for it. Continued fear mongering by right wing political conservatives and self-styled patriot and militia groups, and more of the divisiveness it generates, could cause the pendulum to swing too far left—way left of President Obama.

PRESIDENT OBAMA AND THE U.S. DEBT

Astute political scientists have observed that President Obama did not want to send America further into debt by bailing out banks and the American automotive industry. For the conservative base that loves Sarah Palin to constantly imply that Obama erred in taking these actions is to bury both the problem and its solutions in political rhetoric.

They know better. They know that the economy was swiftly spiraling downward during the last year of the Bush Administration. This was due to Bush initiatives that poured money into defense industry coffers and to financial gambling around the American housing market. Obama had to do what he did. Any American president, no matter what his politics, would have had to.

Republican finger-pointers surely know about the waste in Iraq, which has been documented and publicly mentioned dozens of times. Example: More than $5 billion in American taxpayer funds was wasted on failed infrastructure projects in Iraq, according to audits by a U.S. watchdog agency. Here are but a few of them:[2]

- A $40 million never-occupied prison sits empty because it was unfinished when handed over to Iraq's Justice Ministry and more than $1.2 million in unused construction material was abandoned.
- A $165 million children's hospital goes unused because it has no electricity even though gardeners tend its manicured lawn.
- A $100 million wastewater treatment system is not connected to houses and neighborhood tanks are not joined to the treatment plant and sewage still runs in the streets.
- A $5.7 million convention center hosted a few events, even though its meeting halls were not connected to the main power supply nor was other work finished when the facility was transferred to the Iraqi government. The glass façade is missing from large sections of the abandoned buildings, which have fallen into disrepair.

Palin never mentions that much of the bailout money was a loan. It is to be paid back. During the first quarter of 2010, General Motors turned its first profit in three years. With more good quarters, it may be able to structure a public stock offering as a means of paying on the government loan, which is secured by the U.S. Treasury owning 61 percent of GM.[3] Palin could rack up stacks of credibility if she were more truthful on such matters.

Escalating problems around wars being fought on foreign soil, plus our nearly bankrupt health care and retirement systems and a faulty economic system, could get so bad that only strong government intervention in the form of socialism can solve them. That should not be America's last option.

The question is what if the New World Order gang really exists and is already running the world behind the scenes? In that case, it may be too late for any intervention for the United States. Our nation would then be part of a bigger plan, a formula in which the shots have already been called.

IS SARAH PALIN AUTHENTIC?

"I will live, and I will die for the people of America," Sarah Palin told Tea Partiers at their 2010 convention in Nashville.[4] Was this a drama queen speaking or was it as authentic as any person can get? Is this something she often says to her parents, her spouse, her children, her friends, or was it premeditated as the best way to cap a speech she was paid at least $100,000 to deliver?

Palin's Nashville appearance was a crucial turning point. Some believe it was a result of the crowd chanting "Run, Sarah, Run" that she said she would consider running for president in 2012 "if I believe that this is the right thing to do for our country and for the Palin family."[5]

Since then a rash of Palin 2012 merchandise has been appearing at every rally Sarah attends.

Palin had already made her decision before addressing the Tea Party Convention. "It would be absurd not to consider what it is that I can potentially do to help our country," she told Chris Wallace, host for Fox News Sunday, in an interview which took place a few hours before her Saturday night address at the Tea Party convention but was broadcast Sunday morning. It was all carefully orchestrated.[6]

Some Tea Party sympathizers had split off, not attending the convention because they thought the registration fee and the big bucks for Palin's speech just didn't match Joe six-pack's wallet. Palin's response was reminiscent of the brouhaha about the expensive wardrobe that suited her up for the vice presidential campaign. Then, she promised to give the clothes back. (Does anyone know if she did?) This time Palin said she wouldn't make apologies for taking the six-figure speech fee because she planned to give it to conservative causes. She didn't say which ones would benefit so perhaps it will go into her war chest.

PALIN AS REVEALED IN HER BOOK

Palin's book, *Going Rogue*, is a retort and an image polisher. It addresses nearly every negative thing said about her or attributed to her or done by her during the 2008 presidential campaign. Prominent are reasons or excuses for the gaffs she made when interviewed by Katy Couric. Now she tells us what she reads. It appears to be a carefully prepared laundry list of the white clothes variety. One of Palin's many surprises revealed in the book is that she apparently reads Plato. Well, not really. Lightweights shouldn't attempt to either read or be philosophers. Looking at her book (page 24) and at another Plato quote on her Twitter page, one concludes that she has copied them from some bastardization of Plato's works. They read more like pop culture than Plato.

God and President Reagan have top billing. It is understandable that she wants to identify with Ronald Reagan and predictable that she will constantly remind us of her faith and her prayerful approach to life. Overall, that is admirable, but it does seem a mite overdone in some places.

There are some surprises. Sarah's teen infatuation with show biz celebrities is interesting. She was greatly impressed by the movie stars who made brief campaign appearances with her, and we find out which ones contacted her. Maybe after tasting politics and some celebrity status, Palin will do her country and her ego a favor and opt to become a celebrity. Ultimately, that may be the more lucrative route.

EVOLVING FROM HOCKEY MOM TO WHAT?

If Sarah was at one time living the life of an all-American hockey mom, she certainly isn't now. Fox News has paid to put a television studio in her living room, the Sarah PAC (Political Action Committee) has several political policy advisers on its list of funds paid out, and a Wasilla hometown acquaintance says the Palin home on a nearby lake, where an airplane is often parked in the driveway, has been expanded into a compound.[6]

How does this mesh with her down home image of a loving mom caring more about her children than anything else? When the young'uns come home from school is mom done e-mailing her million-plus Facebook fans, writing newspaper columns, and getting e-mail and phone briefings from several advisers charged with bringing her up-to-speed so she doesn't continue to embarrass herself and her supporters by not knowing how our federal government functions? Is she getting help in such areas as:

- Our nation's political history
- Past and ongoing foreign policy priorities
- Contributing factors to the nation's ongoing recession-inflation cycles
- How the president and White House Office of Management and Budgeting form the federal budget
- What the limits are to the power of the president
- How to delegate both tasks and decision making to cabinet members and agency heads
- What she needs to know from the daily news headlines
- Who to deal with in guiding legislation through sticky Congressional wickets

Then there are the trips. Mother Sarah spent much of 2010 not only scooting between states to help conservative primary campaign would-be winners, but she is also on the roster of the Washington Speakers Bureau, reportedly getting paid approximately $100,000 a pop for speaking engagements.[7]

Assessing Palin's authenticity forces us to look at her self-fashioned image an as antiestablishment conservative and self-defined political rogue. The *New York Times* reported in February of 2010 that this antiestablishment rogue regularly speaks to a bipartisan nobility of Washington insiders who have helped enrich her financially and position her on the national political stage.[8] Bipartisan nobility? Are we back to the New World Order, which has adherents and working members in both political parties? What are we to make of this, coming as it does from a visible critic of the Washington establishment?. Here are some questions:

- Is it an about-face designed to help raise money?
- Is it an early indication that an out-of-the-box presidential candidate might sneak inside the box to promote her ambitious goals?
- How much of a disconnect is this with our corn-fed, Bible-bred, and apple-pie image of Sarah Palin that she has worked so hard to perpetuate?
- Sarah Palin obviously is building a support system, but for what?

Palin has assembled an impressive package of past, and possibly future, political figures with an ability to raise money. To some, this is an impressive accomplishment they think will make her a powerful figure. To others, it is an example of how ambitious she is and to what extent she will go to meet her personal goals.

It has been reported multiple times that a friend once told her, when she was running for mayor of Wasilla, that maybe some day she could run for governor. Her response was that, no, she wanted to be president. We could say wow, but then there is a double wow. Look where she is now.

What conception does Palin have of her power, importance, and abilities? Apparently enough to demand that President Obama fire Rahm Emanuel, his Chief of Staff. She also publicly recommended that Canada dismantle its public health-care system.

This from an Alaskan hockey mom? Well, hockey mom is how she wants us to think of her. That's in one breath. In the next, she wants us to believe that she is capable of running the United States. Goodness, how many hockey moms could, or would want to, do that?

Hockey mom? Forget it. She is no longer a hockey mom. Local folks in Wasilla say they hardly ever see their former mayor. Her crammed schedule has her crisscrossing America, making foreign appearances, while trying to assimilate a daily barrage of incoming advice and out-going messages to supporters; this makes her nearly inaccessible. What about her kids back home in Alaska? Sarah comes from a supportive family and is able to foist the kids off on sister, mother, etc.

Is all of this behind-the-scenes visible political organizing a function of what Sarah Palin called believing that God would present her with the next open door? It seems very worldly for such a divinely inspired path.

SARAH'S U.S. TOUR: CAMPAIGNING?

Within weeks of giving up the Alaska governorship, Sarah hit the road. Did she want to get to know the lower forty-eight or was she campaigning? Maybe both since she should know more about the rest of the United States if she is to ever seek any federal government office.

Sarah targeted twenty of the Democratic Congressmen up for reelection, called it her "hit list"—not divinely inspired language— and gave this list a home on the Web, where the graphics are such that you look at these candidates through the crosshairs of a gunsight. Some think this approach is cute, but others say it belies a lack of respect for our high-ranking public officials; most believe it is in bad taste, but a few say it carries a violent message. In appealing to her fans, there is a line Sarah should not cross. There is plenty of room for dissent in our nation, but no room for igniting peoples' rage to destructive levels. Talking trash or mocking the U.S. president is not in good taste. It is something true patriots do not do in public.

Here's a snapshot view of an early stop on Sarah's road show.
March 27, Searchlight, Nevada, hometown of Sen. Harry Reid, one of the highest-ranking Democrats in Congress. This Saturday night party was probably the biggest Searchlight has ever seen. Country songs and Tea Party rappers revved up the audience, Sarah held the crowd rapt during a desert dust storm.
"We're saying that big government, big debt, the Obama-Pelosi-Reid spending spree is over. You're fired!" she told the crowd. "We're not going to sit down and shut up."
Liar, Thug, Traitor, Commie Usurper read one woman's homemade poster, next to a picture of President Obama as the devil. There in the midst of an obviously angry crowd, speakers denounced Democrats for portraying Tea Party members

as angry and violent. (This four-hour rally was stop one on a three-week tour by the Tea Party Express. It ended April 15, tax deadline day, in Washington with a Tea Party rally.)[9]

SARAH AND THE APPLE

So, has Sarah, like Eve, eaten the proverbial apple or not? If Sarah Palin were to be auctioned off, which piece of the American pie would place the winning bid? (You can call that the winning votes.) Would it be Joe six-pack? What if he thinks he owes his job to the Obama bailout? What if his sister, a single mom, can't afford health insurance for herself and three children? What if he doesn't own a gun and go deer hunting? How about soccer moms? Do they all shop at Wal-Mart? Do they all live in tiny towns in the least populated states? How about feminists? After all, Sarah Palin carved herself quite a career as a "feminist." Whoops, she still refers to women as "ladies" in her book, *Going Rogue*. But then she does call historic feminists Elizabeth Cady Stanton, Susan B. Anthony, and Harriet Tubman heroic figures. That throws a carrot to both feminists and black Americans. (In fact, a lot of carrots are thrown in *Going Rogue*.)

How about senior citizens filled with nostalgia for the good old times? How many cheered when the AARP endorsed the Obama health care plan? Was Sarah tapped by right-wing Republicans? Did they finger her because she had the right image or maybe because they could do a quick makeover or did they just pay the highest price? The key question is how authentic is Sarah Palin? Either Sarah Palin is for real or she is a paid mouthpiece for some political group. If Palin is for real, it would be logical to think she would run for office as a Republican. Maybe she is playing everyone against the middle while she sees if she can raise enough money to go it alone. If Sarah Palin didn't eat the apple and is for real, it may be excusable that she has courted varied constituencies and their leaders simultaneously. Does this mean she might run for president as an Independent in 2012? Were Glen Beck's August 28, 2010 Restoring Honor rally in Washington and his Labor Day rally in Anchorage, Alaska, both with Sarah Palin as companion speaker, a test to see how much support one or both of them could muster as a potential 2012 presidential/vice presidential candidate on an Independent ticket?

The corollary is that as likeable as she may be, she is not qualified for any top governmental post on a nationwide level. Her job experience was as Alaska governor. She quit before her first term was up, probably because she was offered at least $5 million to write a book

Despite the fact that Sarah apparently "remembered" what she had read sometime in between the Katie Couric interview and the writing of *Going Rogue*, Sarah is not well read and knows little about the rest of the world at a time when global issues and how they are handled is increasingly important to the United States.

If Sarah Palin did eat the apple, then she is probably the mouthpiece for a political group. The obvious choices would be the libertarian/Tea Party Movement or right-wing conservatives and the rumored secret group that allegedly runs the world. This latter group may exist only as a conspiracy theory, although some of the arguments for its existence are conceivable.

MASTERMIND BEHIND SARAH PALIN?

By late summer of 2010, it looked as though there was a brilliant mastermind behind Sarah. Her two books (the second scheduled for release the fall of 2010), her Discovery Channel booking for a series on Alaska, her contract with Fox to be a news analyst, her highly paid speaking engagements across America, the transformation of her Alaska home into a complex giving roost to numerous functionaries, and including a TV studio, all smack of a paved route to numerous resources, seed money, and political influence, plus expertise way beyond both her means and intellectual prowess. An inside joke that can be shared: It is completely Rovian!

Even Sarah's book signing tour was planned to make political impact, shrewdly spotlighting her in places where she would draw the most fans and positive visibility. Book tours usually include some major cities, but for the most part this tour sidestepped them. Preference was given to places where there was high unemployment and where she and McCain had done well during their campaign.

If Sarah Palin is a front piece, she may also become a victim. Were she to be elected president of the United States, the voters themselves also could have become victims. If we are involved in a plot to be part of a globalized world, we are all being deceived and used.

Citizens of a democracy have the right to know who their real leader is. As a puppet president, Sarah would not be leading the country. Someone like a Karl Rove, a Dick Cheney, or a Paul Wolfowitz would be behind the scenes calling the shots, but they would also be only paid functionaries assigned to work on behalf of the international business and financial kingpins.

Because conservatives have polarized America, using God or any other name they wish to champion their cause, their ascendancy to power would place the country in jeopardy. Don't believe this? There is also a lot of cunning and unheralded planning involved. It appears that Sarah Palin was being upped as a star before anyone knew this trajectory would be labeled vice presidential candidate.

SARAH PALIN THE ROGUE

Going rogue! Perhaps Sarah's book title is the real clue to her aspirations and the route she will travel in search of the White House. Maybe going rogue means that a determined and somewhat stubborn Sarah will run for office as an Independent, ditching right-wing Republicans, trying to trash the Democrats, and counting on Tea Partiers, disenchanted Republicans, and various fringe groups to vote her into office. What an exciting free-for-all! What a disaster for our country!

Palin is a self-styled rogue. Rogues usually are not team players. Yet, Sarah says that all the important life lessons she learned were from playing team sports, notably basketball, in high school. Rogues often don't work well with other people. They can be headstrong and go off on tangents. They tend to be self-centered. Many intelligent rogues have become successful entrepreneurs because of their tendency to work only for themselves. Others are so erratic that they can't be trusted.

During her campaign for vice president, Sarah demonstrated rogue behavior in her interactions with John McCain's presidential campaign staff. Some of them are highlighted in the book *Game Change* by Mark Halperin and John Heilemann, who imply that Palin was unstable.[10]

This Sarah Palin profile can be verified in *Going Rogue*. Some Palin fans would call it "straight from the horse's mouth." These are some of Sarah Palin's "true confessions":

119

- Impatient with politics
- Never had it in her to play the Republican Party game (in Alaska)
- A jock who couldn't relate to how she thought most cheerleader types lived (many feminists think the cheerleader image is the one she most embodies)
- Calls herself a nerd, but that doesn't mesh with the many hours she devoted to track and basketball
- She was way out of her comfort zone when she entered a beauty contest to earn college scholarship money
- Can't accept the fact that political machines twist and distort public service

Does *Going Rogue* showcase any redeeming qualities for Sarah? Yes, most definitely. Here are some of the outstanding ones:

- Sarah learned many important life skills at an early age from a mother and father who had remarkable parenting abilities.
- She has demonstrated an excellent work ethic from the time she was a teen, whether it be babysitting, working in a diner, hauling fish nets, or giving all she had as a member of the track team or on the basketball court.
- Sarah has always been goal oriented and constantly works hard to achieve her goals.

Does this profile sound like good old-fashioned apple pie? Yes, some of it does.

A GENEROSITY OF GENERALITIES

Palin tends to look at people as general types and not as individuals. Here are two examples from *Going Rogue*:

Page 76: Sarah refers to one of her Wasilla critics as "a Birkenstock-and-granola Berkeley grad who wore her gray hair long and flowing and with a flower behind one ear..." (Sarah has fit this woman into a predetermined group of people that she judges in a negative way.)

Page 95: "Todd's not in management. He *actually* works." (The implication is that people in management don't work. That writes off a big percentage of responsible, patriotic American citizens.)

Until recently, Sarah referred to all states except Hawaii and Alaska as "the lower forty-eight." She also often refers to separate nations as collective pockets of countries.

Such views make it difficult to assess the characteristics—and beliefs—of individuals. On another level, it makes geography a tangled mishmash. More important, it would make it difficult for such a leader to assess input on a variety of options from one's advisers. It also makes it difficult to set foreign policy. An example of this type of thinking is this bumper sticker: *Bring our troops home—Send the Democrats*. How then, do we deal with the Democrats serving in the military? Do we bring them home with the troops and then send them back? Should we just leave them where they are serving, hoping they won't get slaughtered before the reinforcements come? What if we send all the Democrats, and there aren't enough troops to do the fighting? Do we send illegal Mexican immigrants?

Following her campaigning in 2008 and her 2009 book tour, Sarah absorbed more United States geography. She downsized her categories to red states and blue states. She probably knew by name the states in which her twenty targeted congressmen lived during the 2010 midterm elections. Sarah spent most of her travel time during the summer and fall of 2010 shunting back and forth among those twenty targeted campaign regions promoting opposition candidates.

Then there are those troublesome Washington people. Of course if the "McPain" ticket had won, she'd be one of them. Would she still criticize them and write them off them as a group? No, she would probably have to start dividing them up into political parties, or perhaps by whether they were elected officials or long-time civil service bureaucrats.

Palin also frequently contradicts herself. The Republican Party would be really smart to start trying to absorb as much of the Tea Party movement as possible, Palin told delegates to the February of 2010 Tea Party Convention, adding in the next breath, "This is a beautiful movement because it is shaping the way politics are conducted. You've got both party machines running scared." The logic of her statement is far from transparent. If the Republican machine is running scared, then how does Palin propose it be convinced to absorb the Tea Partiers?

SARAH PALIN'S METEORIC RISE TO FAME

How do you explain it? Sarah Palin's meteoric rise to fame…who or what fueled it? She ran for vice president and lost. That was enough in 2008 to relegate her to semioblivion. After Sarah Palin's failed bid for the vice presidency, she was more or less expected to head back to Alaska to serve out her term as governor. This was like putting her in the kitchen with her pots and pans. Her response? Sarah resigned as Alaska governor in the middle of her first term of office. She gathered together her resources to wage a rogue's campaign, but for what? Was it really to declare, at least to herself, that she had not been defeated?

What was it that Sarah Palin shoved in the face of everyone? Was it pizzazz, chutzpah, stubbornness, determination to reach her goals, her ability to draw people to her, her image as a Main Street hockey mom, her homey sayings, her flag-waving patriotic slogans, or a strange combination of circumstances not yet made clear? "[Her] way of speaking in credulous golly-gee may have been off-putting to some, but there is a kind of authenticity there that no image handler could conjure," wrote David Carr in his April 4, 2010 *New York Times* article titled "How Sarah Palin Became a Brand," saying that "In Ms. Palin's America, everyone's got bootstraps; they just need to have the gumption to find them." Carr also cited Sarah's stories about everyday people overcoming great obstacles, her ability to politically come from the outside and rule from the middle, and "her inability or unwillingness to connect with the establishment leaders" as giving her credibility. Carr, however, believes she didn't like "governance," is done with that and wants to be a TV personality. Not everyone agrees with this latter assessment.[11]

With help from somewhere, Sarah became a one-woman national media empress, with book and TV earnings in the millions to show for it. Now even daughter Bristol is becoming a TV personality. Amazing. This is what movie stars and other celebrities do. Who, or what, brought this well-packaged woman from Alaska with a 1950s mentality into this star quality atmosphere?

Many grandmothers of the 1950s may have liked Sarah Palin at first glance, but after a peek under the crust, surely they could see that this wasn't any apple pie they would serve to a guest. Sarah Palin repeatedly characterizes herself as being independent. It is one of the five most repetitive themes in *Going Rogue*. So, will she run for president as an Independent? Watch, wait, and see but get involved in the process way before election day 2012!

THE SUMMING UP

Americans are people of hope but not of blind hope. We are people of faith but not of blind faith. We have, for dozens of decades, been among the most educated, creative, and inventive citizens on the planet, but others are now catching up with us. Worldwide, people of faith and hope still look up to us as pacesetters. Many of them aspire to the freedom and liberty they do not yet have.

This is not an opportune time for America to ignore the output of its brightest and best citizens nor to cease its longstanding commitment to educate its people to the fullest extent possible so that we can continue to be a nation of achievers.

If America is plunged into an era of Palin-inspired antiintellectualism, it risks a future in which more and more jobs are outsourced and the United States could face the emergence of another superpower. It was announced in August 2010 that China had surpassed Japan to become the world's second largest economy and that, at its present state of growth, it would not be long before it was number one. Much of the U.S. debt has been financed by China. In some respects, China holds our destiny in its hands.

The *Guardian*, the British newspaper most read outside of England, said this:[12]

> The figures underscore China's emergence as an economic power that is changing everything from the global balance of military and financial power to how cars are designed. It is already the biggest exporter, car buyer and steel producer, and its global influence is growing.

There is possibly another problem that is much more urgent: Mankind's survival on planet Earth is threatened. Citing the rate at which we are polluting planet Earth, plus the possibility that an asteroid could strike our planet, noted astrophysicist Stephen Hawking warns that in order for humanity to survive, we may have to move from planet Earth to another planet within a century. We are years away from having the technology to do this.[13,14]

We are living at a moment in history in which we have an extraordinary opportunity to define the future course of humanity. What humanity is becomes constantly defined and redefined by both how we describe it and what we do as part of it. We have defined it by our great faiths, by what our spirituality calls us to do. These definitions are the loftiest, the most aspiring we have. They call us to the ultimate peaks of love and compassion.

The difference between our perception of these peaks and how we actually live is the murkier region in which we define by our deeds the humanity we are part of today, this month, this decade. It is more reasonable to assume that the Creator has made all of us—not just a certain group of fundamentalist Americans—his stewards of planet Earth, endowed us with the abilities to accomplish this mission, and counts on us to grow in our understanding of our role in this great global undertaking.

CHAPTER SEVEN

WHAT PIECE OF THE AMERICAN PIE DOES SARAH PALIN HAVE?

"We're not the hippie family who only eats organic and the children meditate and go to school of the arts. But we're not apple-pie and republican either." ~ Leonardo DiCaprio

What is Sarah Palin's constituency? Who would vote for her if she ran for national office? The answers, at this point, are more opinion and projection than solid, hard facts.

Polls conducted in mid-2010 placed the Tea Partiers (TPs) in about the twenty-second percentile of the American electorate. It is safe to say that most of them would vote for her unless she completely unravels between now and the 2012 election. (Pundits claimed in mid-2010 that she definitely would run for president in 2012, but others said she is more interested in seeking a nonpolitical, money-generating celebrity status.)

It helps that the TPs do have an organization that gives them an agenda and rallying issues, as well as a communications network and a proven ability to carry-off rallies that attract thousands of people. That 22 percent figure could be boosted by people from rural America who aren't officially TPs but sympathize with how TPs stand on many issues.

One of the most important factors will be whether or not some relationship between the Republican Party and the TPs firms up. As long as Sarah Palin keeps trashing Washington politicians at rallies there will be a great deal of ambivalence. The Republican Party is not apt to drift away from its current Republican office holders.

The Republican Party has, in two years, strayed way right of center, whereas many Republican voters would like to see a more middle-of-the-road platform.

A THREE-WAY RACE IN 2012?

If the TPs and Republicans don't join forces, then we could be looking at a three-party race in 2012, a thought that strikes fear into the hearts of most Republicans because that split would certainly benefit a more unified Democratic Party. This could mean tolerance of a Republican/Tea Party merger rather than facing Democrats in a three-way split.

It should be emphasized that not all of Sarah Palin's followers are conservative Republicans nor are they all Tea Partiers. Many are from the more radical self-styled patriot groups or the sovereign citizens, who are anti-government.

Democrats then might reach towards middle-of-the-roaders in both parties. It is interesting to note that in the 2010 primaries there was an increase of nonoffice-holding candidates. Were they pinning their hopes on the anti-Washington sentiment?

WOMEN VOTERS

In looking at Palinism, women voters can be sorted into two general categories—those who would vote for Sarah because she is a woman and those who would vote against her because she does not embody feminist ideas. In addition, many professional women do not like Sarah's "dumbing down" of America. For the most part, they are more apt to see through her, so often thumb their noses at her anti-intellectualism.

Many of those who would vote for her because she is a woman are already TP members or sympathizers. Yet, there has been support for Palin from some unlikely quarters. "Conservative though she may be, I felt that Palin represented an explosion of brand new style and muscular American feminism," observed professor and philosopher Camille Paglia," who is also a best-selling author.[1]

There are women who agree that Sarah's self-described pit bull determination and personal story make many women admire her. The

New York Post labeled her "a feminist dream." National Public Radio wants to know if she's the "new face of feminism" and other writers are suggesting that there is a new kind of feminism that she embodies.

WHAT THE FEMINISTS SAY

Women who are self-described feminists would rather see Palin feed her ego by achieving top celebrity status in a nonpolitical venue. They point out that in the last presidential election a high percentage of women voted for Obama. Sarah Palin's selection by McCain as his running mate was interpreted by the media as an attempt to get the vote of women after the elimination of Hillary Clinton in the primaries.

A differing perspective is offered by Malia Litman in her book, *Rebuttal to the Rogue*. McCain, she writes, already had a trophy wife and now he wanted a trophy vice president. (Wonder what Todd Palin thought about that?). In 1980, he had divorced a wife crippled by a 1969 car accident to marry a beautiful Phoenix heiress. Did McCain think a trophy running mate would get him votes because she was a woman? Wrong. Dressing Palin up in trendy outfits and stylish pumps, then expecting her to not give interviews or press conferences, sent a very, very macho and patronizing message to workingwomen across America. Meanwhile, Palin was supposed to appear on stage, keep quiet, and look yummy. She chafed at the bit and then let it all hang out when the race was over.

The Palin candidacy went fairly well at first. An Associated Press voter survey conducted Sept. 5, 2008 found that among white women, 65 percent said Mrs. Palin shared their values, compared with 46 percent who said the same of Mr. Biden. A *Newsweek* poll revealed support for Mr. McCain among white females at 53 percent, compared with 37 percent who favored Mr. Obama.[2]

To some women, McCain's selection of Palin was an insulting slap in the face and definitely not a way to win over supporters of the bright, capable, professional public servant that Hillary Clinton still is. Hillary's supporters wanted to see much more in a candidate than a pretty face, dressed up body, and a mouth that had to be hushed because of the alphabet soup that poured out of it. So, the female vote went disproportionately to Obama and McCain may still not know why. (He had Palin help him campaign in 2010.)

Here is more about the "McPain" fiasco. McCain's daughter Meghan has written her way into prominence. She first wrote a book about her father and interned at *Newsweek*. A bit of a maverick, she describes herself as a woman who despises labels and boxes and stereotypes and is liberal on social issues. Meghan supports same-sex marriage, is prolife, objects to the new Arizona immigration law backed by her father, and is interested in helping craft a more liberal redo of the Republican Party. Sarah Palin brought "drama, stress, complications, panic and loads of uncertainty" to her father's losing 2008 presidential campaign," Meghan reports in her latest book, titled *Dirty Sexy Politics*.[3] Meghan has a get-it-all-out-there writing style that doesn't hesitate to call Palin "the Time Bomb" and places Sarah's selection as her father's running mate on the "line between genius and insanity."[4]

CRACKS IN THE GLASS CEILING

Here are some reactions to the Palin choice from an unnamed writer at eladyland.net, posting a piece called "18 Million Cracks in the Glass Ceiling."

> "No thank you. Feminism is about freedom of choice and her values don't line up with mine. Do you think she's going to fight for LGBT rights? Does she care deeply about rebuilding our badly damaged social safety net and addressing income equality? How about universal health care and fighting for human rights and going after the international slave trade? We can be genuinely proud that Hillary has normalized the idea of a woman running for the office of president of the United States. She's right in claiming that her campaign cracked the glass ceiling. I'll know we've made progress when next time it's not the gender or the race of the candidate that's making headlines, but just the bold and visionary policies they put forward to restore the American dream for all people."

The above direct quote notes some of the polarizing issues, plus the hurdles we have to surmount. Palin talks about the glass ceiling, too. In her Oct. 2, 2008 interview with CBS reporter Katie Couric, when asked by Couric what previous vice president impressed Sarah the most, and why, Palin cited also-ran and defeated Democrat Geraldine Ferraro because she is the one who first shattered part of that glass ceiling. When Couric followed up by asking what actual vice president she admired, Palin's ambition broke through. She replied, "I think those who have gone on to the presidency [like] George Bush Sr. [who] having kind of learned the ropes in his position as [vice president] and then moving on up."

In another installment of the Couric interview, Palin said, "I'm a feminist who, uh, believes in equal rights and I believe that women certainly today have every opportunity that a man has to succeed, and to try to do it all, anyway. And I'm very, very thankful that I've been brought up in a family where gender hasn't been an issue. You know, I've been expected to do everything growing up that the boys were doing. We were out chopping wood, and you're out hunting and fishing and filling our freezer with good wild Alaskan game to feed our family."

THE WAL-MART MOMS

There's nothing wrong with being a Wal-Mart mom, but it is not the best icon for an intelligent, savvy, knowledgeable, experienced professional woman. Feminists sense the difference that Palin doesn't seem to grasp. She doesn't think characterizing herself as a Wal-Mart mom is a handicap in running for the nation's vice presidency. In fact, she's been hung up on that image for just over a decade

In 1999, when a couple who worked at the Wasilla Wal-Mart decided to get married in an aisle of the store, shoppers convened, tour-bus shoppers stopped to gawk and Palin, the mayor, officiated. Afterward, Palin told a reporter she had to hold back tears. It was so sweet, she said. It was so Wasilla. She's right. *It was so Wasilla!* [5]

SHORT TAKES ON SARAH PALIN

Here are some points about Palin and Feminism:
- Sarah Palin is a proud member of Feminists for Life, which tries to convince young women that choice means giving up the right to choose when it comes to choosing when or whether to have a child.[6]

- Some feminists can't accept Palin as a symbol of women's empowerment, but in her book *Righting Feminism: Conservative Women and American Politics*, political science professor Ronnee (sic) Schreiber builds a case upon the premise that conservatism and feminism are not mutually exclusive.[7]
- Feminist Gloria Steinem, who says Sarah Palin is Phyllis Schlafly, only younger, also said, "This isn't the first time a boss has picked an unqualified woman just because she agrees with him and opposes everything most other women want and need. Feminism has never been about getting a job for one woman. It's about making life fairer for women everywhere. It's not about a piece of the existing pie. There are too many of us for that. It's about baking a new pie."[8]
- "Many female critics of Palin, in Washington and New York politics and media, found their careers enhanced through the political influence of their powerful fathers, their advantageous marriages to male power players, and the inherited advantages of capital. The irony is that a Palin, like a Barbara Jordan, Golda Meir, or Margaret Thatcher, made her own way without the help of money or influence," says classicist and historian Victor Davis Hanson.[9]
- "This is fascinating. What we are witnessing is the historic hypocrisy of second-wave feminists. Whether you agree with Governor Palin or not, she is feminism in its truest and purest form. She has found a way to balance work and family the way all women hope to—with the help of a loving family. Sarah Palin is everything the feminists fought for," claims Michelle Bernard, President, Independent Women's Forum.[10]
- "In picking Palin, Republicans are lending credence to the sexist assumption that women voters are too stupid to investigate or care about the issues, and merely want to vote for someone who looks like them," said Ann Friedman, deputy director of the *American Prospect*.[11]

Sarah Palin upset the applecart—no, she cracked the tea party china—when she endorsed Carly Fiorina, former Hewlett Packard CEO, in California's 2010 Republican Senate primary race. Many of Palin's Tea Party supporters, who sided with Fiorina's more conservative rival, Chuck DeVore, were angry. They threw the busted china back at her. Here are some of the comments they put on Palin's Facebook page:

- "Fiorina is a RINO (Republican in name only and we don't need any more of those)."
- "Why wouldn't you back Chuck DeVore?"
- "The REAL CONSERVATIVE is Chuck DeVore."
- "Sorry, Sarah, but I think Chuck DeVore is the conservative candidate you should be supporting. I don't agree with this endorsement AT ALL! What are you thinking Sarah?"

What *was* Sarah thinking? Does she believe she is now head of a new feminist movement and should support women candidates? Is she putting distance between herself and conservatives? Is she sending signals to establishment Republicans? Has someone like Karl Rove crafted a game plan for Sarah? Has she figured out that there is a budding populist movement that is for government and not against it? Or, is Sarah simply a loose cannon?

THE SOCCER MOMS

For many moms, their soccer-playing children are only one aspect of their lives. It certainly isn't what they base their political philosophy on. Not all soccer moms are Republicans or Wal-Mart shoppers or married to Joe six-pack. Many have interests other than sports. Few of them hunt and fish. Some are feminists, and some are not. Being a soccer mom is one part of everyday life for these women. Some are prolife, but some aren't. A few drive pickup trucks, but most do not. Some have a lifestyle similar to Palin's before she became a millionaire, but some do not. Some are Palin supporters and some are not. In other words, being a soccer mom has no direct correlation with being a Palin supporter. It is poor reasoning and illogical to think otherwise.

THE MAMA GRIZZLIES

Sarah Palin's latest stereotyped group is the *mama grizzlies* whom she imagines to be so protective of their cubs that they will want to ensure that America's future, as reshaped by Palin and/or the candidates she backs, will give golden opportunities to this next generation. The mama grizzlies movement, however, has touched off some backlash by a proabortion rights group named EMILY'S list. "Sarah Palin has predicted a rising tide of mothers and women voters who will support her so-called 'Mama Grizzly' candidates," EMILY'S List president Stephanie Schriock said in a news release in August 2010. "Palin has made it her mission to defeat candidates who have worked hard to champion the rights of women and families across the country and replace them with conservative candidates who want to repeal health care, stand with big business, and eliminate a woman's right to choose," Schriock said in asking both women and men to let their voices be heard and "to reject Palin's reactionary candidates and backward-looking agenda." The group put out a Web video and is pushing a Sarah Doesn't Speak for Me campaign. The appeal is aimed at "Democrats, Independents, and moderate Republicans who have no home." The video features women in bear costumes saying how their "cubs" are threatened by the agenda of Palin and candidates she supports. They also discuss the risk of losing health care coverage, abortion rights, and unemployment benefits.

An antiabortion rights group, the Susan B. Anthony List, responded asking EMILY'S List "to come to grips with reality." The "Sarah Doesn't Speak for Me" interactive Web site will solicit and share not only information about what is called "the radical agenda of Palin's candidates," but also personal stories. EMILY'S List claims to have raised more than $43 million to support candidates in the 2007–2008 campaign cycle which included Palin's run for vice president.[12]

A CBS poll conducted in November of 2009 reports that 34 percent felt abortion should be available to those who want it, 40 percent felt is should be available under stricter limits than it now is, and 23 percent felt abortions should not be permitted under any circumstances.[13]

THE JOE SIX-PACKS

The last two years have been hard ones for many of the Joe-six-packs. Some have lost their homes. Many have lost their jobs. If the majority of them are angry and frustrated, Sarah Palin's magnetism may draw them to her. If, however, they recognize that the financial fiasco emanated from the Bush Administration, the backlash could very well drive them into the Democratic camp. An earlier generation of Joe six-packs was primarily aligned with the Democratic agenda.

The mention of Joe six-packs is somewhat difficult because it stereotypes people and offends some people. This is, however, a stereotype invented and defined by Sarah Palin. Like the soccer moms, not every American male in this stereotyped group can be expected to conform to the same religious persuasion, the same lifestyle, or the same hobbies. In fact, they don't all drink beer!

THE ONLINE BIGOTS?

That Sarah Palin's following includes bigots is obvious by the signs they carried and the words they shouted at some of her rallies. Politically, they are even more noticeable online. That Sarah has not publicly denounced them may tarnish her image.

A disturbing online trend is that obvious bigots affix comments to news stories and informative articles, reacting (often with crude and insensitive language) with emotion and little or no reasoning or logic. Here are some examples.

Pakistanis Officials Refuse Scanning: A six-member delegation of Pakistani legislators on a State Department-sponsored tour refused a body scan at Dulles Airport before boarding a flight for New Orleans and reportedly were hailed as heroes when they returned to Pakistan.[14] Senator Abbas Khan Afridi, head of the delegation, told GeoNews they considered the compulsory body scan an insult to parliamentarians of a sovereign country. According to the account of this incident given by GeoNews, they were told in advance of their trip to the United States that they would not face any such discrimination during their visit. The State Department, however, claimed that the delegation was told before leaving Pakistan that they might have to submit to extra body searches the same as randomly selected Americans are required to do.[15] "We are disappointed that the group took offense at the security procedures thousands of Americans and visitors must endure at airports every day," said Larry Schwartz, communications officer at the American Embassy in Pakistan. "No offense was intended. Indeed, they were warmly welcomed at high levels in Washington," Schwartz said. At issue here are some of the comments to the online story by Geo News:[16]

- "I love the effect this is having on Muslims. Every international airport should get priority to keep this Muslim scum out. Hopefully it will keep this trash from coming to the U.N. Brilliant move."
- "The scanners should also have showerheads installed to hose down them stinky dudes before they get on planes."
- "If they are Muslims, scan 'em, strip search 'em, and hose 'em down. You don't want to go through the scan? Don't let the door hit you in the ass on your way out of our country. As far as I'm concerned, those pakis who refused the scan were concealing weapons of some sort."
- "Put the scanners in every airport in this country, and stop all flights from other countries that don't have and utilize the scanner."

One would expect comments on this story to zero in on what appears to be a public relations fiasco giving the U.S. State Department a black eye. Instead, it was the Pakistanis who were at the receiving end. Questions:

- What does Sarah Palin think of these responses?
- Would she write them off as acceptable patriotism?
- Does Palin attract followers of this ilk?
- If she does, are they welcomed as her supporters?
- Does she condone this sort of head set?

Trash Talking: *New York Times* columnist Maureen Dowd covered what she termed a boisterous women-against-Palin rally in Anchorage, Alaska, in early September of 2008. Dowd reported that local radio personality Eddie Burke had lambasted the rally organizers as "a bunch of socialist, baby-killing maggots." No professional in any field would have talked like this a decade ago. Throwbacks to the 1950s some of these Alaska types may be, but nobody talked that way then.

This trash talking is not just an Alaskan phenomenon. Because the Internet, it is nationwide. It carries with it rabid thoughts, poisonous personalities, cesspool mouths, and disrespect for fellow Americans.

"Redneck," Sarah, is a derogatory term! Check your dictionaries for definitions of a redneck. Here are a few: "often disparaging, often a derogatory term, offensive slang, a bigot, has prejudiced, unfair, and unreasonable ideas and beliefs."

At a May, 2010 rally in Charlotte, North Carolina, Palin denied that the Tea Party movement had roots in violence, racism, or rednecks, saying, "I don't really have a problem with the redneck part of it, to tell you the truth." She then read redneck jokes off her cell phone.[17]

Does Sarah not know the definition of redneck or is she really okay around people using derogatory words about other people, being bigoted, and having unfair ideas and beliefs? Does she not care what impression she gives? Few Tea Party leaders, Rand Paul included, would endorse this kind of behavior.

HOW DID THE FRINGE GET SO LARGE?

Some American leaders are trying to convince us that the ignorance and bigotry being expressed in such appalling terms is coming from some fringe groups. Not so, unless our fringe has exploded into several million people.

The truth is that inflammatory language is also coming from high places, with the words only a wee bit more polite. It is even more astounding that Americans are tolerating this trash talk. Leaders in every walk of life should be calling for an end to it. The danger is not just the filthy talk. That's a symptom. The real disease is the anger that is behind these words.

This anger is blatant and is translated into vicious, vulgar language that substitutes profanity and ugly epithets for a reasoned argument. This type of confrontation is disheartening to people who seek enough unity that Americans can begin to do something about *very real problems* that have nothing to do with feuding personalities

Today, in America, apparently being angry means you can get away with saying anything you wish. Meanwhile, people in other English-speaking countries are scratching their heads and wondering how Americans could become so disrespectful of each other.

ARIZONA THREATENS LOS ANGELES

Following passage of Arizona's new immigration law, several U.S. locations threatened to boycott Arizona and its businesses because they considered the law discriminatory. One was Los Angeles, which has a large legal immigrant population. Arizona Corporation Commissioner Gary Pierce, calling the Los Angeles City Council's thirteen-to-one vote to boycott Arizona and its businesses "the silliest boycott," did something that was not silly. It was a deadly threat. He threatened to cut Arizona-based electrical power for Los Angeles.[18]

This action was outlined in a letter Pierce wrote to Los Angeles mayor Antonio Villaraigosa on May 18, 2010. The July record high temperature in Los Angeles is 107 degrees. It got up to 112 degrees during a heat wave in September 2010. The downtown's elderly residents and people with asthmatic conditions can, without air conditioning, become seriously ill in a matter of minutes when temperatures are above 90. In addition, lack of electricity causes fires touched off by people who are careless with candles and falls by people trying to find their way in darkness.[19]

Similar boycotts have been voted on in Oakland and Berkeley, California, as well as in Boston, Massachusetts, Seattle, Washington, and Austin, Texas. Opponents to Arizona's immigration law believe it smacks of racial profiling and encourages discrimination against Mexicans, many of whom legally live in the United States, including in Los Angeles.

Fortunately, Pierce's threat was not carried out.

ARE YOU SURE, SARAH?

Does Sarah really want angry, bigoted, abusive, out-of-control extremists, some of whom want to tear down government structure, as her constituents? Some of these people don't like the game and don't play by the rules. How can she depend on their continued loyalty and support?

What if Sarah decides she needs to make some compromises to make progress with her agenda? What if she tries to rope in some powerful, established Republicans in order to broaden her base? What if these people turn against Palin and make her the butt of their anger?

DEALING WITH EXPRESSIONS OF AMERICAN ANGER

Americans have been angry before and have also faced bad times that had an impact on our ability to find jobs and support families. Such times also elevate the crime level. They understandably fray tempers, exacerbate problems, and cause frustration and desperation. Yet, never before have we listened to such fiery, raw, and disrespectful language. Bad language used to be quashed from the pulpits and in classrooms. Scout leaders and business owners didn't tolerate it. Certain words were rarely heard, not even spoken among friends. Now these words abound in article comments on the internet.

It is as though people everywhere are testing the limits of freedom by being disrespectful. Right after the health care legislation vote Congressman Emanuel Cleaver (D-MO), who is black, was spat upon by alleged Tea Party members. One protestor was arrested and turned over to Capitol Police. Cleaver's office decided not to press charges. Were they being kind or fearful?

There is another sidelight to this story of Republican and Tea Party rage. There is also a very large segment of the American people that is angry because for eight years the most powerful position in the world was given to George Bush, who inherited from the Clinton Administration a relatively peaceful and prosperous country with a federal budget surplus. By a constant series of poorly addressed catastrophes and by his allegiances to the rich and the powerful—read that as the biggest banks, insurance companies, and corporations in the defense industry and elsewhere, President George W. Bush brought the nation into a financial nightmare that was documented long before he left office.

A president elected to respond to that financial nightmare, which is almost an impossible challenge, is constantly under attack, handicapped from doing his job, and is personally attacked with poisonous epithets. What has happened to well-informed constructive criticism?

President Obama needs the informed input, respectful support, and well-intentioned prayers of all the American people behind him to meet this momentous challenge. Who are the real, authentic patriotic Americans? They are the people who will give him this support. Neither the president nor the American people need parties or movements that are against so much. We need to be proposing solutions to problems that if unaddressed, may threaten our future. We need legislators who give up name-calling to respond to the needs of their constituents. We need congressmen who will respond to the president's numerous invitations to give input and reach compromises.

GOVERNING BY EXAMPLE

Leaders of a democracy are expected to govern by example. Instead, some members of the Republican Party are using or condoning disgraceful expressions of an angry public at the expense of our national security.

Republican legislators reportedly stood on a Capitol balcony after the health care vote and held aloft letters that spelled out Kill the Bill. Unidentified sources have reported that the Kill part was raised and held for some time before the rest of the sign was held aloft. Inciting the public in such a manner is reprehensible. When it comes from incendiary actions by elected legislators who are sworn to uphold the U.S. Constitution, it is inexcusable.

Even worse: Members of Congress who voted for the health bill received death threats, some had their office windows smashed, and in at least one case gas lines were cut to homes of their relatives. The cutting of gas lines could have caused deaths but luckily didn't. One hopes these actions have been investigated by the authorities and charges have been made. Shortly after this incident, Congress had to hire extra security for at least ten members of Congress who were subjected to vandalism and death threats. Some think these threats and acts of violence against our own elected officials amount to domestic terrorism.

We have elected officials who are acting like children. Because he didn't like the health care vote, Senator John McCain vowed to quit functioning on behalf of the American people. He said he wouldn't be voting on any legislation the rest of the year. This is like the proverbial "I don't like you anymore. I'm not playing in this sandbox. I am going to take my toys and go home." It is childish behavior and from a man who had run for the U.S. presidency less than three years before.

Republican initiatives to embrace (or failure to denounce) the most volatile, disrespectful and hate-mongering segment of their supporters eventually may not improve their ability to get reelected. The real damage is that it thwarts true political dialogue and impedes attempts at consensus. Eventually this could have an impact on the ability of our elected officials to govern.

How, when such action is desperately needed, are the members of the executive and legislative branches of our government going to be able to tackle the wide array of serious problems confronting us?

Conservative Republicans, the Tea Partiers and others, keep insisting that the will of the people must be recognized. It was. In the 2008 presidential election 53 percent of the American people who voted put Barack Obama in the Oval Office and a Democratic majority in Congress because they wanted change. They wanted health care legislation, curbs on some Wall Street activities, and other changes that have been initiated. It was a negative reaction to Bush's base—the haves and the have mores.

Did Republicans think that tolerating Tea Party activists and their hangers-on that engage in hate rhetoric such as homophobic and racial slurs was an acceptable route to getting votes and a path to the White House? The Democrats aren't gloating. Still reverberating in their ears are the shouts and threats at the Palin-McCain political rallies, with racist signs, placards showing a noose around Obama's neck, and shouts of "Kill him—kill the Muslim!"

This happened in America! Do American citizens have any idea of how these scenes played and were critiqued around the rest of the world? American citizens should be ashamed. In fact, some are so ashamed that they are moving out of the country. It is rumored that the number of American expatriates (many of them retired middle class professionals) has risen during the past two years. It is, however, difficult to find statistics for American expatriates since even the IRS can't keep up with all of them.

OVER THE TOP RHETORIC

One man tried to express moderate and tactful opinions on a conservative Web site. The result? He was called "a commie queer." Isn't that illogical? When people erroneously talk about death panels, use words like Armageddon to scare Americans, and warn of socialism when they don't understand that many Europeans enjoy a good standard of living because their government is socialist, that is unfortunate.

"If Glenn Beck or Sarah Palin or Rush Limbaugh choose to make a living peddling partisan hate and anger and mangled conspiracy theories, there will always be people for them to sell a bill of goods," says Tom Daschle, former Senate Democratic leader. "It is not healthy for our democracy." Daschle accused some Republicans of being more interested in scoring political points against President Obama than caring about the future of the country. He suggested that they are ignoring their legislative duties and instead listening to the chattering conservatives.[20]

In this age, when so much information is easily accessible, it is self-imposed ignorance not to know the truth of matters. If people under a 100 IQ think these erroneous thoughts, that's one thing. For people with a higher IQ, it means they are oblivious to truth because they do not seek it. It also means they do not understand the democratic process.

Democracy is a contest of ideas resulting in a peaceful election followed by the winning candidates and their party governing. It has been this way in the United States for nearly two and a half centuries. American policy, arrived at through the democratic process, is never completely agreed upon by everyone. How could it be?

SARAH PALIN'S ADMIRABLE QUALITIES

It is easy to see why Sarah Palin may have been popular in high school and, later, propelled into a political career by being elected her hometown's mayor. Sarah has perseverance. Once she is determined that something is right, she pursues it doggedly. She has iron-willed strength and lasting power when it comes to implementing or getting something she strongly believes in. Sarah entered the political stream armed with exemplary values that were instilled in her by her parents as part of her upbringing.

Her parents, Chuck and Sally (Sheeran) Heath, deserve much credit for Sarah's early personality, the one that served her well until she brushed shoulders with other character types as she aspired to travel from the Alaska governor's seat to a prized position in Washington. In *Going Rogue* she tells about the sense of fair play that she assimilated while being actively involved in team sports.

Ideally, it would be wonderful if she could pass that sense of fair play on to those of her supporters who are anything but fair because of their hatred of things they don't understand. If she could exhibit a positive role model that convinces onlookers that she does not approve of hate mongering, prejudice, and bigotry, it will serve her well in the long run.

Sarah Palin took a beating in Heilemann and Halperin's book, *Game Change.*[21] Many of the negative charges they raised about Palin and her vice presidential campaign boo-boos can be documented. Some of these can be written off as functions of her naiveté. Veteran political reporters John Heileman and Mark Halperin did not include source notes at the end of their book, as does Bob Woodward, who set the standard for this kind of journalism.

Heilemann and Halperin say some staff members assigned to Sarah by the McCain campaign to prep her for debates discussed the possibility that she was mentally unstable.[22] They also relate that McCain staffers agreed that if he won the election Ms. Palin would have to be relegated, as vice president, to a largely ceremonial role. They also report that these staffers felt that if McCain died or was too sick to continue in office it was inconceivable that the nation be placed under the control of a President Palin.[23]

PROBLEMS THE UNITED STATES NEEDS TO TACKLE

It is hoped that the next presidential race will focus on the very real problems facing America, instead of dissension on such constitution-rattling issues as separation of church and state. Some of those very real problems are:

- Exporting our nation's high tech to China, which now has more modern factories than the United States does.[24]
- Dealing with China as the next emerging superpower when our primary tie is that China holds most of our debt.
- Defusing the volatile hostility in the Mid East by first brokering peace between Israel and Palestine.
- Exploring how we really feel about globalization and trying to determine what the benefits and drawbacks are.
- Deciding whether we are going to spend billions to modernize our outmoded factories and industrial infrastructure or whether we can substitute the outsourced jobs with jobs in the clean energy field and in the presently short-staffed health services sector.
- Investigating ways to downsize our enormous federal bureaucracy by subcontracting to civilian companies, privatizing certain functions, and eliminating duplication and overlapping functions of the several agencies.

SARAH PALIN'S PIECE OF THE AMERICAN PIE

Ultimately, Sarah Palin's piece of the American pie may directly relate to whether or not the old guard neoconservatives and the nascent Tea Party movement have separate pies or share the same one. It is possible that the conservatives may die of their own wounds suggests *New York Times* columnist Charles Blow, indicating that conservatism is on the rise but could easily fizzle because it is fueled by anger and desperation not by ideas. "I am convinced that the right may win the day, but the left will win the age," he writes, "because the right is running an intellectually bereft campaign of desperation and disenchantment, amplified by a recession."[25] His message: Great recessions don't last. Great ideas do.

Should Sarah Palin run for president in 2012, what would her constituency be? Were Sarah to guess, her answer might be a new breed of feminists, the Wal-Mart and soccer moms, the mama grizzlies, the Joe six-packs and most members of the Tea Party, plus the right-wing

Republicans. Members of some of these groups, however, may be on much more shaky ground than she realizes.

Another puzzle is how to appeal to such a diverse base. Some want to dramatically reshape the way America is governed and others do not. Some want to rein in globalization and others don't. Some are supporters of big business and the military industrial complex and others detest everything it stands for.

The cleavage is so disparate that Sarah's best option might be to form a third party and run as an independent. Such a course would be a gamble but it could, indeed, make the fractured Republican Party the odd one out, the one at the bottom of the totem pole.

CHAPTER EIGHT

WE ALL OWN THE RECIPE SO CHECK THE INGREDIENTS

"Millions saw the apple fall, but Newton was the one who asked why."
~ Bernard M. Baruch

The most important person in our apple pie scenario is not Sarah Palin nor Barack Obama. The most important person in this book is not any national leader or celebrity figure. When it comes to the pie, it belongs to all of us. It is *our* America. We pay our taxes and we own it. We vote and thereby we help govern it. This means we have the power to change the ingredients in our recipe. We can add some of this or take away some of that. We want to end up with something very good.

We cannot get the right ingredients mixed together to create the best possible America by calling each other stupid, commies, racist, queers, or any other derogatory name. Nor should we support candidates for public office who use such tactics. The level of hate mongering and scare tactics used in America in recent months is unprecedented. Unfortunately, some of the most influential people in America are involved in this disgraceful behavior. Yes, even U.S. Senators. That tarnishes the office they hold. It makes them disloyal and unworthy of the sacrifices Americans, for over four centuries, have made. This behavior is polarizing, that is, it is dividing our people into factions that are facing off to fight each other. We are behaving so badly that high-ranking people in nations that have been our friends are beginning to wonder if we are what we say we are—the champion of freedom and democracy. Are we still, they ask, the land of the free and the brave?

Some foreign onlookers are amused, some are confused, many are puzzled and even more are concerned. We are not living up to our reputation. We thought we had become a mature nation, but have we?

THE MOST IMPORTANT PERSON IS YOU

The most important person in this book is you, the reader. You, collectively, really do need to take back the country. You, the reader, have responsibility for electing a president who can put together a team that understands the needs of America in the global arena and is equal to the challenges faced by our nation in the twenty-first century. Many thought President Obama could do this. The fact that he is only partially succeeding may be an indication that the power structure, i.e., banks, insurance companies, big oil interests, giant corporations, etc., are probably more powerful than he, or we, thought. In some ways the recent U.S. financial crisis was caused (probably knowingly) by these big power interests. They, and perhaps a complicit Bush Administration, were, literally, robbing us, the citizens. What they may not have realized is that our democratic framework cannot long support this laughing-all-the-way-to-the-bank robbing of the American people.

Republicans have long been more sympathetic, and enabling, to these interests and President George Bush was no exception. He gave tax cuts to the rich (as if they weren't already rich enough) at the expense of the middle class. He waded into a trillion dollar war in Iraq knowing that the military industrial complex, including Dick Cheney's Halliburton, would reap most of the profits. Questions abound. Did he allow Defense secretary Rumsfeld to hire Blackwater, which furnished mercenary soldiers disguised as security personnel, to do dirty work that the official U.S. military dared not do or was he simply never told? (In April 2010 several Blackwater officials were indicted on multiple charges.)

This brings up the question of whether or not presidents are manipulated by a power structure that calls the shots behind the scenes. President Obama probably didn't enter the presidential race knowing he could be manipulated, but once in the oval office he may have gotten his wrists smacked and told if you want to do that, then first you have to do this. (If he wanted to do that because he thought he should for the American people, he may have first had to agree to do this.)

The point here is that there may be a dark side to how our government has made decisions in recent decades. Recent decades means under *both* Republican and Democratic presidents.

Instead of squabbling like little children over who gets the first piece of the pie, we need to join together to save the rest of the pie for us, our children, and our grandchildren. We need to turn our backs on the name callers and hate mongerers. Don't let people get away with he's a slimy queer, Obama's a dark-faced Muslin commie, and all that other garbage.

That is not the American way. It is disgraceful behavior. It is especially obnoxious and immoral when people who are doing this say they are following the example of our founding fathers or claim they do it because they are true American patriots.

What is pouring out of the woodwork across America comes not only from the lunatic fringe, but also from people seething with hatred because America hasn't given them what they want. Their dreams, reasonable or not, haven't come true. Many of these people don't listen to explanations, act more from emotion than reason, and say thoughtless things because they don't like, trust or understand most of what happens around them.

Why the Republican Party would try to woo folks like this or why Sarah Palin would condone, even encourage, their behavior is very suspect. It smacks of getting votes at any cost. It looks like an unpatriotic approach that could only be justified by winning power.

Power should not be the name of this game. The name is supposed to be government. The results of good, responsible government are benefits for its citizens, not benefits for fat-cat corporations and their moneylenders.

FIND FACTS, GET INPUT, AND WEIGH EVIDENCE

Modern communications gives us all access to a wide array of information. What you can do is find facts, get input, think, weigh evidence, decide, and act. These are tools for the responsible, well-informed American patriot. These tools can help convince people who are taken in by hate mongerers, name callers, and people acting upon irrational emotions. Why? Because the information they yield makes sense.

Here is the formula:

- **Find Facts -** Make the most of the resources offered by your local library, check mainstream publications and compare information from authoritative online Web sites. Be sure you are looking for *facts*—not somebody else's opinion.
- **Get Input -** After you have discovered facts, look for contradictory evidence. Compare your facts with those cited in the contradictory evidence. Go back to the library and online sources. This time look for expert opinions.
- **Think -** Contrast your opinions with those opinions you have researched. See what your friends and local officials think. This is discussion time. The more constructive interaction you have with others, the more your mind will be stimulated to think about all the information you have accumulated.
- **Weigh Evidence -** Try to compare and contrast your facts, input, and thoughts with those of others. Evaluate how good the sources for the facts are and how believable and authoritative the opinions of others are.
- **Decide -** Firm up your own thoughts and decide what your position is and where it would be in relation to that of others if a one to ten scale were used. If it is at either extreme, you may want to ask yourself why. Finally, claim your decision. State it out loud in a sentence that begins "I believe" and includes the word *because*.
- **Act -** It is not always necessary to act on the things we research, evaluate, and decide. Sometimes we undergo this process to satisfy our own curiosity, or to make sure we are ready to share our opinions with others. Sometimes we act by asking others if they have undergone such a search for truth or by telling them how we formulate our own decisions. If, however, the subject matter requires you to act, once you have been through this process you will feel more certain, more secure and more confident in what

you do. You will also be more effective in dealing with others. Finally, you owe it to yourself to be a truth seeker.

CASE STUDY 1

Polls show that more than 25 percent of those Americans polled believe President Obama was not born in the United States. Why do they believe this? What facts do they have? Where do we look for answers on this?

Birth, marriage, and death information can be found in a variety of places, including newspapers, church records, and census records. The most common source, however, is public records. These may be at the town, county, or state level, depending on where the event takes place. All official biographies of Barack Obama state he was born in Hawaii. How do we prove that this is true or false? It is verifiable by record (birth certificate available to public) that Barack Obama was born August 4, 1961 in Honolulu, Hawaii, to Stanley Ann Dunham (mother) and Barack Obama Sr. (father). Hawaii had become our nation's fiftieth state in 1959. His mother was from Wichita, Kansas, and his father was from Kenya. His parents met in a 1960 language class at the University of Hawaii, where Barack Sr. was a foreign student on scholarship. Following their marriage, Barack Sr. went to Harvard on a scholarship, and the couple was divorced in 1964.

The director of the Hawaii State Department of Health has confirmed that Barack Obama's birth certificate is, as proscribed by law, on file in that department. In addition, it was the custom at the time for hospitals to report births to newspapers. An announcement of Barack Obama's birth appeared in two Honolulu newspapers. Here is the FactCheck.org. report: "When Barack Obama Jr. was born on August 4,1961 in Honolulu, Kenya was a British colony, still part of the United Kingdom's dwindling empire. As a Kenyan native, *Barack Obama Sr.* was a British subject whose citizenship status was governed by the British Nationality Act of 1948. That same act governed the status of Obama Sr.'s children. Since Sen. Obama has neither renounced his U.S. citizenship nor sworn an oath of allegiance to Kenya, his British citizenship automatically expired on August 4, 1982."[1]

Obama's birthplace has been questioned by conspiracy theorists and ultraconservative Republicans because if he is, by birth, a foreign citizen, that could impact on his qualifications to be president of the United States. However, even if Obama were born in a foreign country to a mother who was a U.S. citizen, as his mother was, he would automatically have U.S. citizenship. Obama ran against Sen. John McCain for the U.S. presidency. McCain was born in Panama, where his American parents lived while his father was on military duty.

The internet furor about his birth certificate being faked, forged, or otherwise rendered inauthentic, spread like wildfire through the blogosphere and beyond. Nobody who posted on this apparently had seen the original birth certificate. None of them offered any evidence that he was born elsewhere. The reaction was partially fueled by a scanned copy released by the campaign while Obama was running for president.

Some of the supposed evidence was:
- There was no raised seal on the certificate. (A seal doesn't always show on a photocopy.)
- There is a strange halo around the letters. (This could be due to a light leak in a photocopier or scanner.)
- No creases from folding are evident in the scanned version.
- The certificate number is blacked out. (The certificate number is 151 1961- 010641.)
- The date bleeding through from the back seems to say 2007, but the document wasn't released until 2008. (The certificate is stamped June 2007 because that's when Hawaii officials produced it for the campaign. The campaign didn't release its copy until 2008, after speculation began to appear on the Internet questioning Obama's citizenship.)
- The document is a certification of birth not a certificate of birth. (That is right. The certification is known as a short-form birth certificate. The long form is drawn up by the hospital and includes additional information such as birth weight and parents' hometowns. The short form has always been accepted by the U.S. State Department as proof of birth for persons applying for passports.

CASE STUDY 2

Polls show that numerous Americans polled believe President Obama is a Muslim. It has also been claimed that while living in Indonesia with his mother and stepfather he attended a Wahabi school that taught radical Islam ideology. It has also been widely reported that he is part of an Islamic plot to take over the United States. Where do we look for answers on this?

Barack Obama's father was a Harvard graduate and British citizen who divorced Barack's mother when Barack Jr. was about four years old. Barack Jr. next saw his father briefly seven years later. The bottom line: There is no indication that the father of President Obama was a Muslim in the 1960s. In addition, Barack did not spend enough time with his father to be influenced by him.

The closest link to any possible Muslim heritage would be through his mother's second husband, who was from Indonesia, which is a Muslim stronghold. Barack's mother, known by Ann, her middle name, married Indonesian student Lolo Soetoro, who was attending college in Hawaii. When Suharto, a military leader in Soetoro's home country, came to power in 1967, all Indonesian students studying abroad were recalled, and Obama and his parents moved to the Menteng neighborhood of Jakarta. From age six to ten, Obama attended local schools in Jakarta, including Besuki Public School and St. Francis of Assisi Catholic School.

CNN has reported that all charges tying Barack Obama Jr. to the Muslim faith are not only untrue but absurd. It sent a reporter to Jakarta to visit both schools Obama attended as a child. The reporter said Besuki Public School (known as SDN Menteng 1) is a local neighborhood school attended by students of various faiths, both then and now. The curriculum does not include teaching the Muslim religion. Similar reports were given by the Associated Press and other media.

During this time of his life, Obama was known as Barry Soetoro, a combination of his childhood nickname and his stepfather's surname. Obama's stepfather was then working for a U.S. oil company.

In 1971, Obama returned to Honolulu to live with his maternal grandparents, Madelyn and Stanley Armour Dunham, and attended

Punahou School, a private college preparatory school, from the fifth grade until his graduation from high school in 1979. These grandparents were white Christians and the young Obama was not exposed to any Muslim influences in Hawaii. As an adult, he has been a practicing Christian, attending church almost every Sunday while he lived in Chicago.

He spoke at length about his Christian beliefs in a 2004 *Chicago Sun Times* interview with Cathleen Falsani. President Obama has not been sneaking into a mosque to pray, reading the Koran, praying to Mecca, or observing Islamic holidays with his family.[2]

Obama's mother returned to Hawaii in 1972, remaining there until 1977, when she went back to Indonesia to work as an anthropological field worker. She had a doctorate in anthropology, and her thesis has been described as a classic, in-depth work. She finally returned to Hawaii in 1994 and lived there for one year before dying of ovarian cancer. The birth certificate of his mother shows that she was born in 1942 at Wichita, Kansas to Stanley Armour Dunham (1918–1992) and the former Madelyn L. Payne (1922–2008). His mother had numerous colonial ancestors,[3] descended from fourteen Revolutionary War soldiers[4] and through her, President Obama is distantly related to seven U.S. presidents and two kings;[5] he also shares some common ancestors with the Bush presidents and Sarah Palin.[6]

These senseless charges against Obama are attempts to appeal to racial bigotry and fear of terrorism. They are similar to statements several years ago that falsely accused Republican John McCain of fathering an illegitimate child by a black woman. Obama often refers to his mother as the dominant figure in his formative years. "The values she taught me continue to be my touchstone when it comes to how I go about the world of politics," the President says.[7]

For those questioning Obama's American ancestry, here is an eye-opener: Of Hillary Rodham Clinton's eight great-grandparents, only one was born in the United States. Half of Barack Obama's were.[8]

In addition, Palin and Obama are distantly related. Both descend from Samuel Hinckley and Sarah Soule, who were wed in England in 1617 and were among the first wave of settlers in Plymouth Colony.[9]

Dozens of white ancestors of both Sarah Palin and President Obama can be traced back to the 1600s in colonial America.

CASE STUDY 3

A hoax Associated Press news story claims that Barack Obama enlisted as an undergraduate at California's Occidental College using the name Barry Soetoro and received a Fulbright Scholarship only awarded to foreign-born students. The fake news story was cleverly written and made the usual claims that taxpayers are being ripped off because Obama was educated on public funds, and that he was not born in the United States. Unfortunately, it was widely circulated on the Internet and then spread by word of mouth to hundreds of thousands of people.

This story never appeared in any real newspaper or on any real news wire service. Was it an April Fool's message, or just plain fooling? The first suspicious clue is that it was dated April 1, 2009—April Fool, everybody!

Come on folks? This one is so easy to prove wrong. You can do it on your computer. Go to the Urban Legends Web site for a list of evidence that the claims are false. Better yet, go to the Occidental College Web site where it is openly discussed. Or, go to the Web site for the Fulbright Program for Foreign Students. For openers, the Fulbright Scholarship, which is part of a U.S. State Department program to make bright young foreigners more familiar with our nation, is available to master's degree and Ph.D. candidates only. (Obama spent the first two years of his undergraduate studies at Occidental.)

Many of Obama's classmates have been quoted in interviews appearing in numerous magazines. They all call him Barack Obama.

The fake, never published news story also claims that a patriotic group obtained Obama's transcript from the college and cites so-called damaging evidence from it. Occidental College, as part of its privacy policy, does not make any transcripts available except to its students, who have to request them and usually use them to accompany applications to other colleges. Since transcripts are not public records, they cannot be obtained through the Freedom of Information Act. Other colleges and universities have similar polices of not releasing student transcripts.

The story also claims the Supreme Court would be hearing a case maintaining Obama was foreign born and thereby disqualified as a presidential candidate. Wrong. Their case docket is a matter of public record. Just go to the official U.S. Supreme Court Web site, look on the left, and push DOCKET. It has a search engine you can use to look for cases and when they are scheduled to be heard.

Other Obama hoaxes traveling the Internet falsely claim that he cancelled the National Day of Prayer, accepted campaign donations from Saudi Arabia and Iran, signed a bill to bring thousands of displaced Palestinians to the United States, said disrespectful things about the American flag, and was sworn into office placing his hand on the Koran.

People who want to learn about Obama's upbringing and his personal thoughts on several subjects should read his two books, *Dreams of my Father* (Three Rivers Press, 2004) and *The Audacity of Hope* (Crown Publishers, 2006).

Again, it is self-imposed ignorance not to check out things which have their origin on the internet. Many of them *falsely* claim to be written by well-known columnists, said by names we recognize, or to have appeared on such TV programs as *Meet the Press* or in widely read newspapers and magazines.

THE COMMON SENSE APPROACH

Many of the people drawn to Sarah Palin for her folksy way of looking at things say she has a lot of common sense. This certainly is a two-sided coin. A reporter, interviewing people who stood in line waiting at one of Sarah's book signing events, noted that people wondering if Ms. Palin would run for president did not have ready answers to what they thought she might do to get the country out of its messes. But, they argued, she has common sense and understands how to run a family and a state. That seemed to be enough.[10]

Such reasoning is way off course. Knowing how to run a family and how to run a world superpower are entirely different. Kids don't fight with jet planes, bombs, and high tech guns. Outsiders rarely jump into the middle of family fights. The Chinese aren't holding their family's loans. Families can set their own financial objectives and don't have to run them through government budget analysts and legislative bodies. Family members are primarily accountable to each other and not to numerous watchdogs or to a constituency who put them where they are. There is a long list of significant differences between running a family and being at the helm of the U.S. government.

Knowing how to run Alaska and the United States also are very different, although the governorship is a step in the right direction. If it were the governorship of New York or California, it would be a more valuable preparatory experience. Still, governors who reach the Oval Office have to confront such issues as nuclear proliferation, ongoing wars on foreign soil, global climate change, and China's rise toward superpower status.

Would you place the world's future in the hands of a woman who said the Obama administration's nuclear policy was "a lot of smoke and mirrors" because it is difficult to actually build a nuclear facility?[11] Sorry, Sarah, but even if they are difficult to build, they do exist in many corners of the world and it is that existence we must deal with.

Heading the Alaska state government does, however, present unique challenges, one being that its sparse population is spread out over an area more than one-sixth the size of the United States. In addition, the federal government is Alaska's largest landowner. It owns about 50 percent of the land within Alaska's borders.

AMERICANS SHOULD BE OUTRAGED

Americans should be outraged that irresponsible people dare try to influence citizens with falsified information. They should be angry with themselves for believing lies told by people who claim to be patriotic. Far from being patriotic, these rumor spreaders are being subversive and that is, in effect, a dangerous attack on our country.

Whether or not one identifies with, or personally wishes to support, an American president, it is unpatriotic to indulge in spurious, unwarranted verbal attacks. Yes, Americans have freedom of speech, but the norm is for it to be respectful, honest, and responsible speech.

Why do people start these vicious rumors? They do so because they want to divide the people, prey upon such fears as distrust of the Muslim faith, and make citizens fear their leaders. They want to slowly break America's government into pieces they can take over one by one. They count on people to dumbly follow as sheep.

Proof that Americans are indeed being those sheep is in the great numbers of people who believe these outrageous claims, then spread them to their friends. This certainly isn't the route to re-building our country in a way that makes our government more responsive to the needs of its people. Instead, it is a dangerous path that could lead to internal strife.

War within our country could be far more devastating to the freedoms of our democracy than any war we are fighting in Afghanistan or Iraq. Some of the people doing the most talking now, including Sarah Palin, think we should go to war with Iran. That certainly would be a budget-busting scenario. Instead of waging external wars under the platitudes that we are bringing democracy and freedom to people in the Middle East, we should be honoring and preserving democracy and freedom in the United States. We can't give to others what needs to be redefined in the United States.

WHITE HOUSE WORDSMITHS

The reality of White House language manipulation during the Bush Administration was reported in 2004 by respected journalist Ron Suskind in the *New York Times Magazine*. Here is Suskind's account of what an unnamed administration official told him.[12]

"The aide said that guys like me were in what we call the reality-based community, which he defined as 'people who believe that solutions emerge from your judicious study of discernible reality.' I nodded and murmured something about enlightenment principles and empiricism. He cut me off. 'That's not the way the world really works anymore,'" he continued.

The official said, "We are an empire now, and when we act, we create our own reality. And while you're studying that reality, judiciously, as you will, we'll act again, creating other new realities, which you can study too, and that's how things will sort out. We're history's actors, and you, all of you, will be left to just study what we do."

In a nutshell, the above message from the Bush White House was whatever we say (the government) because we say it, it is true. We create our own reality. Do with it whatever you (the citizens) wish. (Like, shove it.)

There is an opposite scenario from the Obama White House. Commenting openly about the furor touched off by a Muslim group that wants to build a mosque near ground zero, President Obama correctly commented that the group has a right to build the mosque because we have religious freedom in the United States. He also noted that the decision to build a mosque close to where the September 11 attack took place might not be wise. That is a fairly simple statement. The president reminded us that our Constitution calls for freedom of religion and said that, in this case, it might not be wise for a Muslim group to build at that New York City location.

The response to his remarks was outrageous. Here President Obama was, defending our Constitution, and people claimed he was supporting the building of a Muslim mosque. President Obama pledged to support the Constitution when he took his oath of office. It was within his presidential duty to remind Americans that our Constitution calls for freedom of religion.

The unusual thing is that several Republican congressmen condemned Obama and twisted his words to mean that he supported building the mosque. No, he supported freedom of religion!

How ironic it is that many Republicans and many of Sarah Palin's supporters want us to return to a simpler form of government in which the Constitution is the governing document, yet when it is convenient, they forget what is in it.

CAUSE FOR CONCERN: THE VANISHING AMERICAN MIDDLE CLASS

In the United States and many other countries the middle class has been a stabilizing factor, filling in the gap between the powerless poor and the rich powerbrokers. Its members could be found in rural, suburban, and urban environments. They covered a large income range and were more numerous than the rich upper-class citizens. The middle class was literally in the middle of a socioeconomical hierarchy, and its members commonly bolstered consumerism and the ranks of property owners. Its members were variously described as white collar workers, meaning professionals, managers, and senior civil servants. The middle class was also the ladder of upward mobility for people in the lower class. Because of this, there were levels of lower middle class and upper middle class. People in the lower class could obtain an education or professional training and move into the lower middle class by starting a small business. If their business was successful, they or their children might become the average middle class.

Now a strange phenomenon is taking place. The American middle class is rapidly diminishing, even as the middle class in emerging countries is rapidly multiplying. For example, the point at which the poor start entering the middle class by the millions is the time when poor countries get the maximum benefit from cheap labor through international trade, before they price themselves out of world markets for cheap goods. In February of 2009, the *Economist* announced that over half the world's population now belongs to the middle class, as a result of rapid growth in emerging countries. Between 1990 and 2005 the middle class in China grew from 15 percent to 62 percent of the population. A similar increase is underway in India.[13]

The diminishing middle class in America is an anomaly. Some of the decline is traceable to the economic recession that saw house and stock values dip by about 50 percent. Other contributing factors are the decline of American manufacturing, the outsourcing of jobs, downsizing during the recession and the elimination of small family owned retail businesses because of competition from discount chain stores.

Here are some scary statistics from the *Business Insider* as posted July 15, 2010 by blogger Michael Snyder.[14]

- 83 percent of all U.S. stocks are in the hands of 1 percent of the people.
- 66 percent of income growth between 2001 and 2007 went to the top 1 percent of wealthy Americans.
- 43 percent of Americans have less than $10,000 saved for retirement
- More than 1.4 million Americans filed for personal bankruptcy in 2009; this was a 32 percent increase over 2008.
- For the first time in U.S. history, banks own a greater share of residential housing net worth than all individual Americans put together.

- In 1950, the ratio of the average executive's paycheck to the average worker's paycheck was about 30 to 1. That ratio has exploded to 300-500 to 1.
- As of 2007, the bottom 80 percent of American households held about 7 percent of the liquid financial assets.
- The bottom 50 percent of U.S. income earners now collectively own less than 1 percent of the nation's wealth.
- In the United States, the average federal worker now earns 60 percent more than the average worker in the private sector.
- The top 1 percent of U.S. households owns nearly twice as much of America's corporate wealth as they did fifteen years ago.
- The average time for an American to find a job has risen to a record 35.2 weeks
- For the first time in U.S. history, more than forty million Americans are on food stamps; the U.S. Department of Agriculture projects that number rising to forty-three million in 2011.
- This is what American workers must compete against: In China a garment worker makes about 86 cents an hour, and the Cambodian worker makes about 22 cents an hour. Approximately 21 percent of all U.S. children are living below the poverty line —the highest rate in twenty years.
- Despite the financial crisis, the number of U.S. millionaires rose 16 percent in 2009 to reach 7.8 million.
- The top 10 percent of Americans now earn about 50 percent of the national income.

Sobering statistics? Yes, and here is what is making Americans victims. Wealth and power are moving to the top echelon, the middle class is being wiped out, and big international corporations with a global base are making piles of money. Why not? What corporation with loyalty to its stockholders is going to pay the American worker ten to twelve times what the foreign worker is willing to work for?

Beware Tea Partiers. Beware followers of Sarah Palin. Representatives of these giant corporations may be pulling political strings behind the scenes and financing the campaign to get your votes. They do not have your interests at heart.

WHO AMERICANS ARE

Americans are people of many races, religions, colors, and creeds. Behind us are those who have gone, and before us those who will come. We look back to our mothers and fathers and all our ancestors. In front, we try to see our sons and daughters, and the sons of sons and daughters of daughters for eons to come. As we feel, so have they felt and will feel then, now, tomorrow, and forever. We are links in a long human chain with a prehistoric past and a misty future. My parents' grasped their parents' hands. Their hands were in mine, and all up and down the line that stretches from time-that-was to time-that-is and time that-is-yet-to-be, we hold each other and create these links, generation after generation. We found we were one, made in the image of a Creator. (Paraphrasing a passage from *How Green Was My Valley*, by Richard Llewellyn.)

Don't believe everything you hear. Try to define for yourself what patriotism really is. Check sources, including the numerous ones mentioned in this book. You own the recipe. You contribute the ingredients. Important chapters in America's story can be written by you. Keep your spirituality, your religion, in your hearts, in your homes, in your church, but remember that America's earliest founding fathers warned about letting it be part of our government. Pray that our citizens, our leaders, and our country may be richly blessed.

Watch out. Sarah Palin didn't get where she is now by having facts in her toolbox. Put them in yours. Be careful. Be vigilant. Be everything you can be.

A NEGATIVE POLITICAL ATMOSPHERE

There are some scary politics in the atmosphere. When Obama and McCain were campaigning for the presidency there were few scare tactics being used. Yet, shortly after Obama took office, there was discernible hate mongering on the horizon. A little over a year later, a nonpartisan, independent polling organization's survey of 2000 Republicans revealed the following: 39 percent thought the president should be impeached; 42 percent believed Obama was born in the United States, 36 percent said he wasn't, and 22 percent were not sure; 63 percent identified the president as a socialist, and

31 percent agreed with the statement that Barack Obama is a racist who hates white people; 25 percent believed the president wants the terrorists to win; 53 percent believe Sarah Palin is more qualified for the presidency than Obama; and 23 percent say their state should secede from the United States.[15]

The questions and their answers give rise to questions like how patriotic is it to want to secede from the United States? The survey also built the following profile of these self-identifying Republicans.[16]

- Most support the death penalty
- Most oppose allowing openly gay people to serve in the military, marry, or teach in public schools.
- They oppose sex education
- They support religious education in public schools
- They believe abortion is murder
- They think only Christians go to heaven.

LET'S GET EDUCATED

Self-identified Republicans believe they are definite, zealous advocates of freedom even though some of their beliefs, if taken a stage or two further, would interfere with the freedom and rights of other people as defined in the U.S. Constitution.

Some of these responses indicate a lack of knowledge in the sense that the respondents had not bothered to do basic research in support of their opinions. Some people confuse socialism and communism. They are not identical nor is socialism a police state. The most common Western civilization definition of socialism is a state run by the government for the people. The governments of Austria, Denmark, France, Germany, Norway, and Great Britain all include aspects of socialism, some more than others. For the most part, their citizens enjoy a high standard of living, their officials are elected by a democratic process, and none can be described as a police state.

Some Obama detractors have also accused him of being a Nazi. Strong words. Where do they come from? Many of these misconceptions are from the mouths of Rush Limbaugh and the like. Actually, right wing conservative fundamentalists are more fascist than left wing liberals. What have Americans been learning in school during the past six decades?

TRASHING OBAMA

There is every reason to believe that if Barack Obama is a foreign-born racist socialist who hates whites and sympathizes with terrorists, then this all would have been proven long ago and the Democratic Party would not have supported him as a presidential candidate. How widespread was this character assassination? Not only has it been spread all over the internet, but it also found a niche in the Republican Party. Scandal around a seventy-two-page document outlining Republican scare tactics to be used to raise party funds broke after it was given to Politico.com the first week of March 2010. The document came from a hotel where a GOP fund-raiser was being held. The strategy involved making people afraid of the Obama Administration by warning donors of "The Evil Empire." It portrayed Nancy Pelosi as Cruella DeVille and Harry Reid as Scooby Doo. It also included the maniacal whiteface image of Barack Obama as the Joker who is a sinister Batman character. The Joker image also turned up at conservative and Tea Party Rallies.[17]

This deliberate trashing of the president received substantial criticism for its racist overtones. Such incidents certainly are more racist than anything advanced by the Obama Administration and put the shoe back on the right foot. Republican leaders doing damage control said this sort of thing happens all the time! Well, if it does, then double shame on them. This Republican National Committee plan also promises donors the funds will save the country from trending toward socialism.

We wonder where does Sarah Palin stand on these scare tactics and character attacks? She said in *Going Rogue* that she learned the best life lessons from being involved in high school team sports. Those did include a sense of fair play and no punches in the gut, didn't they? It should be made clear that shortly after Sarah's "don't retreat, just reload" rhetoric was widely criticized, Sarah said she was not advocating violence. "We know violence isn't the answer," she said, stating that "When we take up our arms, we're talking about our votes."[18]

BRIT TOSSED FROM OFFICE BECAUSE OF CAMPAIGN LIES

There is, perhaps, something we can learn from the mother country our colonial forefathers rebelled against. There you can get tossed out of office for lying about your opponent during a campaign, as England's politician Phil Woolas recently discovered. A Labour Party incumbent, Woolas won the May 6 parliamentary election by 103 votes.

Woolas had accused his opponent of getting support from Muslim militants favoring violence. A British court ruled on Nov. 5, 2010 that Woolas had gone too far in distorting his opponent's positions and said British election law had been violated.. The court ordered that he be removed from office.

Could that happen in the United States? Not likely. Our First Amendment guarantees freedom of speech, even to liars and deceptive politicians, and so this great freedom of ours can be abused by the people who lead our country. That means it is left to voters, not courts, to sort fact from fiction during heated political campaigns. That is even more reason why we need to do our homework. That job has been given to us by our Constitution.[19]

WHAT IF?

How far right can we go before right is wrong?

If a sixteen-year-old who deliberately mows down two policemen stopping his dad's van for a routine traffic stop can be considered a hero by Americans who claim they are part of a patriot movement, our country is in trouble.

It's not a giant step to go from there to several worst-case scenarios. Asking "what if?" is a healthy thing to do. Here are some "what-ifs" disturbing liberal intellectuals.

- What if the New World Order first nurtured decades ago by Rumsfeld, Cheney, Perle, and Wolfowitz now operates on a global level, and its representatives want the U.S. government under their thumb?
- What if it really is the right-wing intelligentsia who are manipulating a takeover of the U.S. government to

disembowel it, so international corporations can be freed of regulatory restraints?
- What if all the financial industry giants and world's largest companies are already operating in a transitional New World Order and globalization mode?
- What if wealth and power interests now want to unseat the U.S. government and disable American democracy?
- What if Sarah Palin is being used by these interests because she can rally the masses behind a false "take back the government" campaign and start a revolution that can be blamed on the patriot movement and its militias while the real instigators smirk and get ready for the next phase?
- What if genocide could occur by doing away with Social Security, Medicaid, and Medicare and rounding up leftist rebels?

None of this sounds like the America most patriotic citizens want to live in, and it certainly may not be in the works. What is true, however, is that we cannot go back to the simpler life of the 1950s because the world has become much more complex in the last fifty years. Yet, most Americans are not satisfied with the status quo.

SARAH PALIN'S PIECE OF THE AMERICAN PIE

There are major questions that need to be answered before the 2012 presidential election, especially if Sarah Palin is either running herself or endorsing and supporting candidates, as she did in the 2010 midterm primary and general elections. Here they are:

- Is Sarah Palin being used as a tool by powerful moneyed interests to round up votes for a right wing agenda that would benefit large international corporations and their financial networks?
- If Sarah is such a tool, is she a very clever woman who is knowingly deceiving members of the Tea Party and "patriot groups" who want to make a downsized government more responsive to their needs or is she instead a naïve victim who doesn't understand the game?

- Why are neoconservative Republicans and Tea Party members courting people with radical, extremist views and trying to normalize some of those views?
- Where are the voices of mainstream America and to whom do they belong? Why aren't we hearing more from middle-of-the-road centrists?
- If Sarah Palin could be duped by powerful people tied to an elite global power network, could American voters again become victims of vested interests who don't care about the well being of ordinary citizens?

"If anyone could make Christian theocracy smell like apple pie, Sarah Palin could," writes Sam Harris in a *Newsweek* September 20, 2008 article titled "When Atheists Attack."

What is Sarah Palin's piece of the American pie? The answer that first comes to mind is that she is stirring up carefully selected ingredients and preparing to bake her very own pie. It may not come out of the oven until 2012. We have yet to see how many Americans will like and enjoy it.

POSTSCRIPT

Sarah Palin's book, *Going Rogue: An American Life*, has been frequently quoted in this book. It is, perhaps, appropriate to say a few things about it. The book was written in about two months shortly after Sarah resigned during her first term as governor of Alaska. Palin signed a multimillion-dollar contract with HarperCollins Publishers.

Although Palin is a college graduate with a major in journalism, she worked with another writer on the book. Her collaborator was Lynn Vincent, senior writer and former features editor of *World*, an evangelical magazine.[1] Vincent has written six books and hundreds of magazine articles. Memoirs are her specialty. She has brought word power and drama to books describing the life of an illiterate former sharecropper, a millionaire art dealer, a special forces commando, a Grammy-winning recording star, and a former Muslim terrorist. Lynn Vincent is a talented writer who now has two best sellers to her credit.[2] She is also known as an opponent to abortion and gay rights and a neoconservative who advocates young-earth creationism.[2]

In discussing her book, Palin reportedly told the Associated Press the following: "There's been so much written about and spoken about in the mainstream media and in the anonymous blogosphere world, that this will be a wonderful, refreshing chance for me to get to tell my story, that a lot of people have asked about, unfiltered."[3] Palin, of course, is widely known for her inability to control language.

NOTES

CHAPTER 1

1. Allen Metcalf and David K. Barnhart, *America in So Many Words: Words That Have Shaped America* (Boston, MA: Houghton Mifflin Company, 1997) 30, 43.
2. *Cambridge International Dictionary of Idioms* (Cambridge: Cambridge University Press, 2002).
3. Palin, Sarah, *Going Rogue: An American Life* (New York, NY: HarperCollins, 2009) 3.
4. Ibid., 66.
5. Wikipedia, "The 1950s." Accessed June 17, 2010. http://en.wikipedia.org/wiki/1950s.
6. Ibid.
7. Palin, 33.
8. Wikipedia, "The 1950s."
9. Ibid.
10. Ibid.
11. Maureen Doud, "Barbies for War!" *New York Times*, September 16, 2008.
12. U.S. Census Bureau, Accessed June 16, 2010. http://www.census.gov/population/pop-profile/2000/chap02.pdf,.
13. The Association of Religion Data Archives, State Membership Report, Alaska, Denominational Groups, 2002. Accessed June 16, 2010. http://www.thearda.com/Archive/Files/Descriptions/RELLAND2.asp,
14. Rosemary Bachelor, the author, was part of a Pulitzer Prize-winning team of Gannett Group newspaper reporters who wrote a series of newspaper articles titled "On the Road to Integration." She also covered race riots in Plainfield, New Jersey, mentored an African American journalism student who became a Washington reporter,

and wrote a series of articles on Plainfield (NJ) area residents who were executives of numerous companies headquartered in New York. She was born in Benton Harbor, Michigan, where she often visited relatives in the 1950s. In all of these contexts she had first-hand knowledge, experience and involvement in issues of the civil rights era.

15. Wikipedia, "Selma to Montgomery Marches". Accessed June 18, 2010. http://en.wikipedia.org/wiki/Selma_to_Montgomery_marches.

16. Ibid.

17. *The American Experience* "Eyes on the Prize, the Story of the Movement." PBS. Accessed June 18, 2010. http://www.pbs.org/wgbh/amex/eyesontheprize/about/pt.html.

18. *Census 2000 Demographic Profile Highlights*, U.S. Census Bureau. Accessed May 27, 2010. http://factfinder.census.gov/servlet/SAFFFacts?_event=Search&geo_id=&_geoContext=&_street=&_county=wasilla&_cityTown=wasilla&_state=04000US02&_zip=&_lang=en&_sse=on&pctxt=fph&pgsl=010&show_2003_tab=&redirect=Y.

19. Lyndon B. Johnson, in a speech to a special joint session of Congress, March 15, 1965, "Special Message to Congress," Lyndon Baines Johnson Library and Museum, http://www.lbjlib.utexas.edu/johnson/archives.hom/speeches.hom/650315.asp.

CHAPTER 2

1. Palin, 22.
2. Ibid.
3. Palin, 28.
4. Ibid.
5. Palin, 394.
6. Barry Lynn, *Piety and Politics: The Right-Wing Assault on Religious Freedom* (New York, NY: Three Rivers Press, 2007) 1-14.
7. Phil Donahue, review of *Pity & Politics: The Right-Wing Assault on Religious Freedom*, by Barry W. Lynn, hardcover edition (New York, NY: Three Rivers Press, 2007) back cover.
8. Nadine Strossen, review of *Pity & Politics: The Right-Wing Assault on Religious Freedom*, by Barry W. Lynn, hardcover edition (New York, NY: Three Rivers Press, 2007) back cover.

9. David Domke and Kevin Coe, "God and the Oval Office: Bush's Brand of Christianity," *Information Clearing House*. Accessed June 19, 2010. http://www.informationclearinghouse.info/article7953.htm,. and David Domke and Kevin Coe, *The God Strategy: How Religion Became a Political Weapon in America* (New York, NY: Oxford University Press, 2008).

10. Chip Berlet, "What Is Dominionism? Palin, the Christian Right and Theocracy," *Huffington Post* , September 5, 2008. Accessed May 5, 2010. http://www.huffingtonpost.com/chip-berlet/what-is-dominionism-palin_b_124037.html.

11. Ibid.

12. Andy Birkey, "God's Army: A Short Guide to Sarah Palin's Extreme Religious Worldview," *Minnesota Independent*, October 2, 2008.

13. Dr. Welton Gaddy, "The Car Wreck That Is Sarah Palin and the National Day of Prayer," *Religion Dispatches*, April 22, 2010.

14. Ibid.

15. Ibid.

16. Ibid.

17. Ibid.

18. Ibid.

19. Ibid.

CHAPTER 3

1. Kate Zernike, "Palin Responds to 'Run, Sarah, Run,'" *New York Times*, February 8, 2010.

2. Mark McDonald, "Palin Speaks to Investors in Hong Kong," *New York Times*, September 23, 2010.

3. Ibid.

4. Richard Duncan, *The Dollar Crisis: Causes, Consequences, Cures* (Singapore: John Wiley & Sons, 2003)

5. CLSA Asia-Pacific Markets. Accessed July 22, 2010. https://www.clsa.com/index.php.

6. The National Association of State Budget Officers' Fiscal Survey of States, Spring 2008, Table A-16. Accessed May 24, 2010. http://www.nasbo.org/Publications/FiscalSurvey/FiscalSurveyArchives/tabid/106/Default.aspx.

7. Ibid.

8. Beth Bragg and Megan Holland, "State Budget May Mean High Times in Anchorage," *Anchorage Daily News*, April 17, 2008.

9. Ibid.

10. Ibid.

11. Ibid.

12. Ibid.

13. California Legislative Analyst's Office. Accessed July 22, 2010. http://www.lao.ca.gov/laoapp/main.aspx.

14. Peggy Fikac, "Texas Legislature Focuses on Education in Budget," *Houston Chronicle*, May 25, 2007.

15. Danny Hakim and David Herzenhorn, "School Aid Fight Erupts in Albany as Budget Passes," *New York Times*, April 2, 2007.

16. United States Federal, State, and Local Government Revenue, Fiscal Year 1955. Accessed June 22, 2010. http://www.usgovern-mentrevenue.com/yearrev1955_0.html.

17. William J. Rand, MD, Testimony before the Senate Committee on Labor and Human Resources, Subcommittee on Labor regarding the causes of decreasing quality of health care under managed care arrangements; Feb. 14, 1994; Nov. 20, 1994; 103rd Session of Congress.

18. Ibid.

19. Carol Finch specializes in health and retirement issues, including advisories on the 2010 Affordable Care Act: list of articles at http://www.suite101.com/profile.cfm/carolfinch

20. Ibid.

21. Mark Silva, "Sarah Palin: Obama's Health Care 'Evil,'" *Chicago Tribune's* Washington Bureau online, August 8, 2009. Accessed July 26, 2010. http://www.swamppolitics.com/news/politics/blog/2009/08/sarah_palin_obamas_healthcare.html.

22. Tom, Moroney, "Palin Tells Tea Party Rally in Boston to Fight Obama," Bloomberg Businessweek, April 14, 2010. Accessed July 26, 2010. http://www.businessweek.com/news/2010-04-14/palin-s-boston-rally-with-tea-party-fails-to-draw-senator-brown.html.

23. "Sarah Palin's Alaska to Air on TLC (The Learning Chanel)," Discovery Communications Press Release, March 18, 2010. Accessed May 24, 2010. http://corporate.discovery.com/discovery-news/.

24. Stelter, Brian, "Palin to Star in a Documentary Series about Alaska," *New York Times*, March 26, 2010.

25. Press releases issued September 26, 2007 and August 4, 2008 by the Alaska Governor's Office.
26. Governor Palin's January 15, 2008 "State of the State Address" to the Alaska Legislature.
27. "Gubernatorial Candidate Profiles," *Anchorage Daily News*, October 29, 2006.
28. Palin, 18-19
29. Heritage Foundation. Accessed July 27, 2010. http://www.heritage.org/Issues/Welfare/Welfare-Spending.
30. "Gubernatorial Candidate Profiles," *Anchorage Daily News*, October 22, 2006.
31. K. Hopkins, "Little Play," *Anchorage Daily News*, August 6, 2006.
32. "Gubernatorial Candidate Profiles," cited above.
33. Press release issued February 11, 2008 by the Alaska Governor's Office.
34. Jessica Yellin, "Palin's Town Charged Women for Rape Exams," CNN, September 22, 2008.
35. Jason Linkins, *Huffington Post*. Accessed May 23, 2010. http://huffingtonpost.com/2010/04/30/palin-event-requires-medi n _558640.html.

CHAPTER 4

1. Palin, 66.
2. Frank Rich, "The Axis of the Obsessed and Deranged,'" *New York Times*, February 27, 2010.
3. Ibid.
4. Ibid.
5. Company Profile for Halliburton, Zeno Bank. Accessed June 20, 2101. http://zenobank.com/index.php?symbol=HAL&page=quotesearch"http://zenobank.com/index.php?symbol=HAL&page=quotesearch.
6. Halliburton Web site. Accessed June 20, 2010. http://www.halliburton.com/AboutUs/default.aspx?navid=966&pageid=2458.
7. "Halliburton Opens Corporate Headquarters in the United Arab Emirates," Halliburton press release. March 11, 2007. Accessed June 18, 2010. http//www.halliburton.com/default/main/halliburton/eng/news/source_files/pressrelease_2007.jsp.

8. Seymour Hersh, "Shackling the President." Seymour Hersh is a legendary investigative journalist and his remarks at the Geneva conference were videotaped. One of those videos was aired on Pakistani TV and can be seen online. Accessed August 15, 2010. http://www.pakistan.tv/videos-current-state-of-investigative-reporting-%5ByRWYa7XHMO0%5D.cfm.

9. Teddy Davis, "Tea Party Activists Unveil 'Contract for America,'" ABC News/Politics , April 15, 2010. Accessed August 15, 2010. http://abcnews.go.com/Politics/tea-party-activists-unveil-contract-america/story?id=10376437.

10. Vinson & Elkins Law firm, Company profile. Accessed August 15, 2010. http://www.vinson-elkins.com/.

11. Davis, cited above.

12. Ibid.

13. Ibid.

14. Vinson and Elkins, cited above.

15. CBS News Senior White House Correspondent Bill Plante interview of Rand Paul on "Washington Unplugged," May 19, 2010.

16. Ibid.

17. Ibid.

18. Domenico Montanaro and Abby Livingston, "Romney Wins CPAC Poll Again," NBC News online, March 2009.

19. Liz Sidoti, "GOP's 2012 Hopefuls Rail Against Washington: Ron Paul Wins Presidential Straw Poll at Conservative Conference," Associated Press, February 20, 2010.

20. Southern Republican Leadership Conference, 2010 Straw Poll Results from SRLC. Accessed June 22, 2010. http://www.srlc2010.com/srlc/srlc-2010-straw-poll-results/

21. Libertarian Party Platform, adopted at May of 2010 convention, St. Louis, Missouri. Accessed June 22, 2010. http://www.lp.org/platform.

22. Jane Mayer, "Covert Operations: The Billionaire Brothers Who Are Waging a War Against Obama," New Yorker, August 30, 2010.

23. Koch Industries Web site. Accessed August 10, 2010. http://www.kochind.com/.

24. Mayer, cited above.

25. Ibid.

26. Ibid.

27. Ibid.
28. Transcript of "Bill Moyers Journal," aired on PBS, April 30 2010, full transcript available on PBS Web site. Accessed May 28, 2010. http://www.pbs.org/moyers/journal/04302010/transcript2.html.
29. Jim Hightower Web site. Accessed May 28, 2010. http://www.jim-hightower.com/node/7285.
30. Moyers, cited above.
31. Edward C. Kirkland, *Industry Comes of Age: Business, Labor and Public Policy, 1860–1897*, (New York,NY: Holt, Rinehart and Winston, 1961)
32. Joseph Gusfield, *Symbolic Crusade: Status Politics and the American Temperance Movement* (Urbana, IL: University of Illinois Press, 1963) 20.
33. Robert Miller Worth, "A Centenary Historiography of American Populism," *Kansas History,* 16, 1(1993): 54-69.
34. Moyers, cited above.
35. Halliburton press release, cited above.
36. Moyers, cited above.
37. Ibid.
38. Ibid.
39. Ibid.
    Common Dreams Web site. Accessed June 23, 2010. http://www.commondreams.org/.
40.
41. Ibid.
42. Ibid.
43. Lyndon B. Johnson, in a speech to a special joint session of Congress, March 15, 1965.

CHAPTER 5

1. "Bush Relatives for Kerry," Democracy for America, July 16, 2010. Accessed July 28, 2010. http://www.bushrelativesforkerry.com/.
2. Ibid.
3. Ibid.
4. Ibid.
5. "Thoughts on Patriotism," *The Nation, Special 125th Anniversary Edition,* July 15, 1991.

6. Department of Homeland Security, "Rightwing Extremism: Current Economic and Political Climate Fueling Resurgence in Radicalization and Recruitment," in-house report dated April 7, 2009.
7. Ibid.
8. Ibid.
9. Dan Harris, "Deadly Arkansas Shooting By 'Sovereignists' Jerry and Joe Kane Who Shun U.S. Law," ABC News/Politics , July 1. 2010. Accessed July 16, 2010. http://abcnews.go.com/WN/deadly-arkansas-shooting-sovereign-citizens-jerry-kane-joseph/story?id=11065285.
10. Ibid.
11. Ibid.
12. Ibid.
13. Ibid.
14. FBI report, official FBI Web site, April 13, 2010. Accessed July 8, 2010. http://www2.fbi.gov/page2/april10/sovereigncitizens_041310.html.
15. Ibid.
16. Ibid.
17. Ibid.
18. Ibid.
19. Ibid.
20. Southern Poverty Law Center (SPLC). Accessed July 12, 2010. http://www.splcenter.org/get-informed/intelligence-files.
21. Ibid. http://www.splcenter.org/get-informed/intelligence-files/ideology/neo-nazi/active_hate_groups
22. "Rage on the Right," Intelligence Report, Spring 2010, Issue Number: 137, Southern Poverty Law Center. Accessed July 8, 2010. http://www.splcenter.org/get-informed/intelligence-report/browse-all-issues/2010/spring/rage-on-the-right.
23. Ibid.
24. Jim Garamone, "Islam Growing in America, U.S. Military," American Forces Press Service, October 4, 2010.
25. Muslim Military Members organization, July 8, 2010. Accessed September 22, 2010. http://www.muslimmilitarymembers.org/.
26. Garamone, cited above.

27. Dan Ephron, "The Guard Who Found Islam," *Newsweek*, March 21, 2009.
28. John P. Avalon, "Muslims in the Military'" *New York Sun*, April 21, 2006.
29. Ibid.
30. Garamone, cited above.
31. Ibid.
32. David Carr, "How Sarah Palin Became a Brand," *New York Times*, April 4, 2010.
33. Ibid.

CHAPTER 6

1. U. S. Senate discussion of the national debt and related budgetary and tax matters, April 6, 2000, 4837, and "The Very Bad Debt Boxscore," testimoney by Sen. Jesse Helms, April 12, 2000, 5381, the Congressional Record, Vol. , 5381, Vol. 146, Part 4, *Congressional Record*, Proceedings of the 106th Congress, Second Session.
2. "Report: U.S. Wasted Billions in Rebuilding Iraq," Associated Press wire story, August 29, 2010.
3. "GM Reports First Quarterly Profit in 3 Years," Associated Press wire story, May 17, 2010.
4. Kate Zernike, "Palin Responds to Run, Sarah, Run," *New York Times*, February 8, 2010.
5. Ibid
6. Mark Leibovich, "Palin, Visible and Vocal Is Positioned for Variety of Roles," *New York Times*, February 5, 2010.
7. Ibid.
8. Ibid.
9. Kate Zernike, "Palin Rallies Tea Party Crowd in Nevada," *New York Times*, March 27, 2010.
10. John Heilemann and Mark Halprin, *Game Change* (New York, NY: HarperCollins, 2010).
11. David Carr, "How Sarah Palin Became a Brand," *New York Times*, April 4, 2010.
12. David Teather, "China Overtakes Japan as World's Second Largest Economy," *Guardian*, August 16, 2010.

13. "Move to A New Planet, Says Hawking," British Broadcasting Corporation (BBC) November 30, 2006.
14. Hunter Stuart, "Stephen Hawking to Human Race: Move to Outer Space or Face Extinction," *Huffington Post*. Accessed November 8, 2010. http://www.huffingtonpost.com/2010/08/06/stephen-hawking-to-human_n_673387.html.

CHAPTER 7

1. Camille Paglia, "Fresh Blood for the Vampire, *Salon*, September 10, 2008.
2. Jennifer Harper, "Palin Triggers Feminism Reversal," *Washington Times,* September 17, 2008.
3. Meghan McCain, *Dirty, Sexy Politics* (New York, NY: Hyperion, 2010) 115.
4. Ibid., 130.
5. Amanda Coyne, "Sarah Palin's Wasilla, Alaska: Where the Bars Are Open Till 5 A.M." *Newsweek*, September 13, 2008.
6. Ruth Rosen, "Election 2008: Sarah Palin and Feminists For Life," History News Network, Aug. 29, 2008. Accessed May 6, 2010. http://hnn.us/roundup/entries/53912.html.
7. Ronnee Schreiber, *Righting Feminism: Conservative Women and American Politics* (New York, NY: Oxford University Press, 2008)
8. Gloria Steinem, "Wrong Woman, Wrong Message," *Los Angles Times*, September 4, 2009.
9. Victor Davis Hanson, "Sarah Palin, Victim of Elitism?" video, ForaTVn. Accessed July 14, 2010. http://www.youtube.com/watch?v=4ywF1-NYYes.
10. Michelle Bernard, "The Sarah Palin Effect:Shattering the Glass Ceiling," Independent Women's Forum, November 10, 2008. Accessed July 14, 2010. http://webcache.googleusercontent.com/search?q=cache:751koD-TzYQJ:www.iwf.org/news/show/20860.html+Barnard+Palin+glass+ceiling+Nov.+10+2008+http://www.iwf.org&cd=1&hl=en&ct=clnk&gl=ca
11. Ann Friedman, "McCain's Sexist VP Pick," *American Prospect* online, August 29, 2008. Accessed July 14, 2010. http://www.prospect.org/cs/articles?article=mccains_sexist_vp_pick.

12. Brian Montopoli, post titled "Sarah Palin Attacked By 'Mama Grizzlies' from EMILY'S LIST" to CBS News' Political Hotsheet, July 15, 2010. Accessed August 17, 2010. http://www.cbsnews.com/8301-503544_162-20013844-503544.html
13. Sarah Dutton, "Opinions About Abortion Remain Remarkably Steady," CBS News, December 8, 2009.
14. Jane Perlez, "Upset By U.S. Security, Pakistanis Return Home As Heroes," *New York Times*, March 9, 2010.
15. Ibid.
16. "FATA Delegation Says No to Scanning at U.S. Airport, Returns Home," posted on U.S.S. Post (United States Online News) March 7, 2010 and referencing a Geo News story broadcast in Pakistan.
17. Mike Baker and Phillip Elliott, "Palin at NRA Annual Meeting Says Obama Would Ban Guns if He Could", Associated Press Writers, May 14, 2010.
18. Emily Friedman, "Arizona Fights Back Against Boycott Threats Due to Immigration Law," ABC News, May 19, 2010.
19. Ibid.
20. Chuck Raasch and Kathy Kiely, "Daschle Accuses Romney of Flirting With Nuclear Anarchy," *USA Today*, July, 19, 2010.
21. Heilemann and Halperin, *Game Change* (New York, NY: HarperCollins, 2009).
22. Ibid., 401.
23. Ibid., 416.
24. For more information on this, see Keith Bradsher's article "China Drawing High-Tech Research From U.S." *New York Times* online edition, March 17, 2010.
25. Charles M. Blow, "Liberals in Limbo," *New York Times*, May 15, 2010.

CHAPTER 8

1. FactCheck.org. Accessed September 7, 2010 (FactCheck.org is a project of the Annenberg Public Policy Center of the University of Pennsylvania. It is a nonpartisan, nonprofit consumer advocate.) http://www.factcheck.org/elections-2008/born_in_the_usa.html.
2. Cathleen Falsani, "The God Factor: Interview With Barrack Obama," *Chicago Sun Times*, April 5, 2004.

3. Rosemary Bachelor, "Obama Ancestry: Part of the Great Melting Pot," Suite 101.com, September 1, 2008. http://www.suite101. com/content/obama-ancestry-part-of-the-great-melting-pot-a66882.

4. Rosemary Bachelor, "President Obama Descends from 14 Revolutionary War Soldiers," Suite. 101.com, September 17, 2010. http://www.suite101.com/content/president-obama-descends-from14-revolutionary-war-soldiers-a287470

5. Rosemary Bachelor, "How Obama Is Related to 7 Presidents and 3 Kings," Suite 101.com, June 13, 2009. http://www.suite101. com/content/how-obama-is-kin-to-7-presidents-and-2-kings-a124948,

6. Rosemary Bachelor, "How Obama, Bush and Palin Are Related," Suite 101.com, June 13, 2009. http://www.suite101.com/content/how-obama-bush-and-palin-are-related-a124832.

7. Tim Jones, "Barack Obama: Mother Not Just a Girl From Kansas: Stanley Ann Dunham Shaped a Future Senator," *Chicago Tribune*, March 27, 2007.

8. Rosemary Bachelor, "Hillary Clinton Has Few American Born Ancestors: Secretary of State Nominee is English, Welsh, Scottish, French and Dutch" Suite 101.com. Accessed September 10, 2010. http://www.suite101.com/content/hillary-clinton-has-few-american-born-ancestors-a81471

9. Rosemary Bachelor, "How Obama, Bush and Palin Are Related" cited above.

10. Kate Zernike, "Enthusiasm for Palin and Echoes of 2008 Divide,'" *New York Times*, November 21, 2009.

11. Brian Montopoli, "Sarah Palin Fires Back at Obama: Mocks His Experience on Nuclear Issues," CBS News, April 10, 2010.

12. Ron Suskind, "Faith, Certainty and the Presidency of George W. Bush," *New York Times* magazine section, October 17, 2004.

13. John Parker, "Special Report: Burgeoning Bourgeoisie," *The Economist* online, February 2009.

14. Michael Snyder, "The Middle Class in America Is Radically Shrinking" *Business Insider* . July 15, 2010. Accessed September 22, 2010. http://finance.yahoo.com/tech-ticker/the-u.s.-middle-class-is-being-wiped-out-here's-the-stats-to-prove-it-520657. html?tickers=%5EDJI,%5EGSPC,SPY,MCD,WMT,XRT,DIA,

15. Poll conducted by Research 2000, a nonpartisan independent pollster; those polled were self-identified Republicans.
16. Ibid.
17. Ben Smith, "Exclusive: RNC Document Mocks Donors, Plays on 'Fear,'" Politico online, March 3, 2010. Accessed April 28, 2010. http://www.politico.com/news/stories/0310/33866.html
18. Jeff Zeleny, "Differences Set Aside, Palin Lends McCain Aid," *New York Times*, March 26, 2010.
19. Brooks Jackson, "A Tough Penalty for False Political Claims," Nov. 5, 2010. Accessed November 8, 2010. http://factcheck.org/2010/11/a-tough-penalty-for-false-political-claims/.

POSTSCRIPT

1. Motoka Rioch and Dave Itzkoff, "Palin Proves to Be a Fast Writer," *New York Times*, September 29, 2010.
2. Lynn Vincent biography, Wikipedia. Accessed November 5, 2010. http://en.wikipedia.org/wiki/Lynn_Vincenthttp://en.wikipedia.org/wiki/Lynn_Vincent.
3. "Sarah Palin memoir to come in 2010," *USA Today*, May 12, 2009.